SO-EGS-189

Playboy's Guide to Rallying, Racing, and Sports Car Driving

PLAYBOY'S GUIDE TO RALLYING, RACING, AND SPORTS CAR DRIVING

WILLIAM NEELY

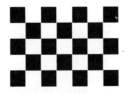

WIDEVIEW
BOOKS

Copyright © 1981 by William Neely.

All rights reserved. No part of this book may be reproduced, stored in a retrieval system, or transmitted in any form by an electronic, mechanical, photocopying, recording means or otherwise, without prior written permission of the author.

Manufactured in the United States of America.

First edition.

Wideview Books/A Division of PEI Books, Inc.

Library of Congress Cataloging in Publication Data
Neely, William.
    Playboy's guide to rallying, racing, and sports car driving.
    1. Automobile racing. I. Playboy. II. Title.
GV1029.N38 1981   796.7'2   81–50335
ISBN 0–87223–726–5 (pbk.)   AACR2

To my father,

who started my lifelong

love affair with the automobile.

And to my mother,

who put up with it.

Contents

Acknowledgments

The following automotive experts and companies supplied assistance and advice which proved invaluable, and I thank them:

Bob Bondurant, Bill Mitchell, Bob Sharp, Dave Ammen, E. Paul Dickinson, Carroll Shelby, Bill Cooper, Chuck Dressing, John Champion, Mitch Williams, Jan Zuijdijk, Serge Haraboski, Koni Shocks, Meon, Inc. (Phoenix Tires), The Goodyear Tire & Rubber Company, Champion Spark Plug Co., Saab-Scandia, Accel, A/T Engineering, Hooker Industries, Valvoline Oil Co., Holley Carburetor, Sports Car Club of America, ANSA Exhaust, American Honda Motor Co., Volkswagen of America, Electrolert, Inc. (Fuzzbuster), Recaro, Tire America, Golden Wheel (Enkei), SEV Corp. (Cibie, Marchal), AutoWorld, Lecarra Steering Wheels, B.F. Goodrich, and BMW.

Playboy's Guide to Rallying, Racing, and Sports Car Driving

Introduction

Way back in the 1940s, when I was growing up, the automobile was king. My earliest recollection of an automobile, I mean a *real* automobile, was a Duesenberg a guy in the next town owned. It was a thing of sculptured beauty, of great, racy fenders with spare tires affixed to one end and running boards to the other. A lot of people still drove cars like that then, but a lot more drove modified Fords and Chevys. And they drove like absolute madmen—at least, the people I hung out with did.

I can remember one night in the back seat of a 1941 Chevrolet two-door, one of the first of the new breeds *without* running boards. I was only a kid but the "older guy" driving—he must have been all of 17—had mastered, at that tender age, the finer art of back-road racing. It went something like this: You found the *most* impossible stretch of road, which was a task in itself because they were all impossible. But you found this really tricky section of road and drove right to the limit, using all sorts of homey, self-taught techniques.

Each driver had his own bag of tricks—which, distilled down to their essence, simply meant he drove the hell out of the car, often white-knuckled.

There were no special handling packages, or even special tires for that matter. You used Firestones because Firestones were what they used at Indianapolis, and if they could advertise that sort of thing in *Collier's* and the *Saturday Evening Post,* it had to be the way to go. To not believe that, for chrissakes, would be like not believing in Norman Rockwell or Sal Hepatica. But on this particular night, my hero driver was right there at the wheel of this gleaming black Chevy with a 270 Jimmy (GMC) engine and every accessory available from the local auto parts store, which wasn't all that much then—fender skirts, steering-wheel spinner, a few chrome parts, and a foxtail on the radio antenna.

I remember vividly how each of the tires screamed a different tune as we careened through the turns of that twisting, bumpy section of U.S. Route 19, between Jane Lew and Clarksburg, West Virginia. It was just after World War II, and we were living.

At the time, I was convinced that this was about the best anybody could have driven that 18-mile section of primitive concrete highway: 18 miles in 15 minutes, and even today, I'm sure it was close to it. It would have taken at least a seasoned whiskey-runner with a load of West Virginia moonshine to match it. It was good driving; it's just not what we today would consider *polished.* They didn't know anything about apexes of turns and diminishing radii and unsprung weight. Hell, all they knew was that if you went through Dead Man's Turn at anything over 50 you crashed. Simple.

I guess what it was was another era. People drove by the seat of their pants. And they crashed a lot. It was expected. But they developed a particular driving style that was hard to beat. Some of them went on to the race track, but most of them just got older and bought a station wagon. "Ol' Vernon's finally grew up," they would say as they sat round the stove in my father's hardware store. It wasn't exactly that Ol' Vernon grew up; hell, his wife made him *sell* the '40 Ford coupe with the Edelbrock heads and the twin Stromberg carbs and the Smitty mufflers, and she picked out a nice flamingo and white Ford Skyliner or a baby-blue and white Chevy Bel-Air with Power Glide, and that was it for Ol' Vernon and the road racing. Many a misspent youth came to that sort of end.

What happened to the rest of us spelled the absolute end of big block *back*-road racing, but it kept us in the high-rev league a lot longer. We discovered sports cars. In most cases it was an MG-TD or a Triumph TR-3, but a few were lucky enough to latch on to a good used 120 Jag or a Porsche Speedster, and they were the ones to be envied. Racing has always had its caste system. It gave the rest of us something to shoot at. And we quickly forgot the techniques of keeping the '41 Chevys and the '40 Fords on the road. Our attention turned to cars that *handled.* Suddenly it was obvious to us that displacement wasn't the complete answer: How else could one explain how a tiny Porsche could run through Dead Man's quicker than the fire-breathing 120M Jag? Our newfound sophistication told us the answer was simple. Handling.

Sure, it's all changed now, particularly the automobile and the cost of motoring. And the speed limit. But from time to time, I see a TD or a Speedster that somebody has restored and I long for the 1950s and '60s when I was a member of this big fraternity where everybody who was driving a foreign car waved to everybody else who was driving one. It didn't matter what kind of foreign car you drove, we were all brothers under the skin. Now, every so often, from my hilltop farm overlooking the town where I grew up, my thoughts go back to Square One; I hear the unmistakable sound of burning rubber and the throaty roar of a really hot big block engine down there on Main Street. The sound pierces the darkness. It's a sound that still makes me hold my breath and cock my head just the slightest bit. It sounds an awful lot like black thunder. And I always remember that '41 Chevy. I miss the racing of my youth.

This book is not about any of that—big block road cars or vintage sports cars. It's about how one can enjoy racing and spirited driving the *proper* way. In our overregulated days. Even without breaking the law. For this, I attended the Bondurant School, just, I said, "to brush up on my technique, and to learn the proper terms for what I had been doing all my life." To my absolute amazement, I learned right off that I had been doing a lot of things improperly all my life. After I completed the course I considered myself (1) a better driver, and (2) lucky to have survived this long.

This, then, is a book about the proper way to drive a race car, as recommended by Bob Bondurant and his outstanding school; and about how to modify a sports car or sport sedan, as suggested by Bob Sharp, who himself was a champion and who today builds some of the most successful cars in Sports Car Club of America racing, and by Bill Mitchell, who is the dean of beefing up and smoothing out the handling and performance of Detroit's current road beasts. It is also a book about solo competition—the name SCCA gives to what we used to call gymkhana or autocross—as experienced by E. Paul Dickinson, five-times U.S. champion and the man who has never been beaten in national competition. It takes a look at road racing, with suggestions from another national champion, Dave Ammen, who shares views with Oscar Koveleski, himself a former champ.

Included are suggestions from some of the top authorities on handling and performance—the people who make Phoenix tires, Koni shocks, ANSA exhaust systems, Champion spark plugs, Hooker headers, Cibie and Marchal lighting, Recaro seats, Momo and Lecarra steering wheels, as well as the experts at A/T Engineering and a lot of other people who helped make the project car a sort of little BMW—which is as good as you can get. If you can come even close to a BMW by modifying an already fine car like the Honda Accord, you are doing damn well. And we can still drive it to the store. Economically. It may prove that Washington hasn't completely legislated the automobile away from us. It still is possible to get a thrill from a small bore-engined car and to compete against the clock or other cars, and to do it on a limited budget.

That's what this book is about.

Maybe it's a *primer* of racing, rallying, and autocrossing seen through the eyes of a West Virginia boy who "grew up" but avoided the station wagon and the Power Glides, and rediscovered the thrill of spirited driving—even with gasoline prices up and cubic inches down.

I hope the book gives you some pointers or improves your technique or inspires you in some way. Even if it simply gives you an *insight* into high performance driving, it may be worth the price of admission. Researching it sure was.

1

Selecting the Car and the Arena

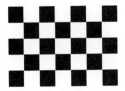

There is no *one* car that is perfect for all forms of automotive competition. Rule One.

In fact, you won't find anywhere a list of the approved ones. Because nearly any car, properly prepared and placed in the hands of a competent driver, will do the job nicely, thank you. So that's exactly what this book is about: the properly prepared car in the proper hands.

Assuredly, there are some cars that are better than others and some that are ready to go, right off the showroom floor. But not many. Almost all cars, sports cars and sedans alike, can be improved upon both for performance and handling. And certainly that's true of most drivers. It boils down, then, to determining (1) what form of competition interests you, and (2) how much money you have to spend. The trip to the winner's circle is, to a degree, predicated upon dollars. Rule Two.

There has to be a checkered flag for some, whether it be road racing, rallying, or solo (autocross) competition; while, for others, the mere thrill of driving fast and well on that favorite stretch of back, winding highway is enough. Driving fast doesn't necessarily mean driving insanely down the road. It means driving *spiritedly* down the road. There's a difference. The latter should indicate that the car is under control. And you *can* bring the thrill back to driving, even at legal speeds.

It takes the proper techniques, knowledge of your car, and a lot of practice to excel at any type of high-performance driving, and there are certain aspects of *precision* driving that are common to all. Each requires certain specific techniques that make that one form unique in driving style, and we will deal with each one in detail later on. For now, let's take a cursory look at the machine in general.

A successful car in competition is, first of all, *competitive*. Obvious? Well, a lot of people don't know what it takes to make a car competitive. Horsepower alone certainly isn't the answer. Richard Petty once said, "It's not the fastest car that wins races, it's the quickest car—the one that goes as fast through the corners as it does down the straightaways." He said it well.

On the other hand, all the genius in the world can't take an uncompetitive car to the winner's circle. The car has to be right in the first place. Skill behind the wheel can help, to be sure; but in the final analysis you must have the right tool for the right job. The effort will fall short if you have chosen a big, hulking sedan for solo or an ill-handling car for road racing. I watched as A.J. Foyt put a relic of a dirt-track car on the pole at Milwaukee a few years ago, when everybody else in the field was driving sophisticated, rear-engined Indy cars. He led the race for several laps, simply through a combination of courage and absolute driving genius, but finally he couldn't hold off the much faster cars. He finished fourth, no mean feat considering what he had to give away in speed and handling. But there are few, if any, A.J. Foyts among us, so we have to have the right machine going in, if we expect to come out even close to the front of the pack.

For openers, purchase a car—or build one—that *can* win in the class or type of competition you have chosen. Since your hard-earned dollars have to feed the beast, what you buy and where you compete will be determined by how much you spend in the first place.

An excellent place to start is in the Sports Car Club of America's Showroom Stock series. Cars for this class are designed as street cars, with no changes at all except for safety equipment. Buying one of these cars gives you a chance to see if you are really going to like competitive driving—without actually purchasing a race car or a vehicle so poorly adapted to highway driving that it must be towed to the track, driven, and then put away until the next race. You can drive the showroom stock car to work on Monday morning. You can even enter it in autocross or rally events for additional driving experience.

Even showroom stock cars must be meticulously prepared, because you can't win unless you're around at the finish. It is more important to have a car 100 percent mechanically and safely prepared than it is to have one that is the hottest thing on the track but has been thrown together. Sheer power often takes precedence over durability and handling. But sheer power seldom wins for any driver in any race.

Of course, it won't help much if you have a good handling and well-

A Renault Le Car leads a pack of IMSA racers through a turn at the Champion Spark Plug Challenge.

prepared car if you don't understand what it is doing, so you must prepare yourself as well as the car.

A sports car or any finely prepared car is very much like a thoroughbred horse. You just don't spend $30,000 on a thoroughbred and keep it out in the pasture and ride it occasionally; nor do you work it in the field like a plow horse. You take it out and you exercise it and you run it, or else it goes to seed. Well, your car won't necessarily go to seed, but your feel for it will.

Whether you choose one of the stock categories or simply want to improve your own car for highway driving, the only extras you'll need are the proper tires, shocks, and stabilizer bars, which you should have anyway to fully enjoy a car and to make it safer on the highway. But even these changes will require you to drive more attentively, particularly if you want to get the thrill of fast, tight driving, so you must continue to "work out" your thoroughbred.

Certain cars tend to have what the learned who have gone to places like the Bondurant School refer to as "oversteer" and "understeer" characteristics. These terms refer to the attitude of the car when you go screaming into a turn. (Later we will spend as much time discussing these characteristics as any single aspect of handling.) Too much over- or understeer can be bothersome, if not downright awe-inspiring, so many beginners are told to look for a "neutral handling" car for starters. A neutral handling car is one that doesn't feel as if the front end *or* the back end is sliding toward the wall as you enter a turn.

A race driver once described understeer as "hitting the wall with the front of the car" and oversteer as "hitting it with the back of the car." Succinct but accurate. He also said that "there's no such thing as a *neutral* handling

9

Car & Driver *magazine's showroom stock Mazda RX-7.*

car." And he was assuredly right about that too. "Neutral handling" is a term that is thrown around loosely in racing.

Generally speaking, the sporty type car is a lot closer to neutral handling than the average American sedan, and even certain imported sedans are closer to neutral. Again, in general, any mid-engine car tends to be neutral handling—X1/9 Fiats and 914 Porsches and Ferrari Dinos are three that fall into this category, as do most Porsches, simply because these cars are almost always pretty well balanced.

There are so many variables as to how a particular car handles that the only way to really get to know it is to take it out in the automobile pasture and run it. And practice. You'll quickly learn what it takes for your car. These variables make it difficult if not impossible to come up with a definite list of "perfect cars" for particular situations. Certain drivers, for example, have a tendency to make a car oversteer or understeer because of the way they drive. To a degree, at least, you can produce either characteristic as a result of your driving technique. There are people who literally attack a corner, charge at it with the brakes locked up, and then turn the wheel and go around the corner. That type of action is bound to induce a form of understeer, at least going into a turn—even in a Porsche.

Selecting the Car and the Arena

You can clearly see this principle demonstrated in Formula One competition, where you have two cars that are theoretically identical team cars, and yet halfway through the race one driver has burned the front tires off his car, while the other driver runs the whole race without changing rubber. Formula cars are close to being balanced, or neutral, so they all should get through an entire race without a tire change. But if one driver slams the car into the corners and throws the wheel, he will turn a "neutral" handling car into one that understeers. He will push the front tires sideways so much that they will heat up and burn up.

Without any more sidestepping of the question of which is the best car, I can only point to the most successful ones. The winners. But, even with such a list, it is difficult to determine just how much of that success is a result of superior driving and/or preparation. At any rate, here are the cars that won the most races in SCCA and IMSA (International Motor Sports Association) racing, rally, and solo competition (eliminating, specials, and formula cars) in the past two years:

MG Midget, Triumph Spitfire, Fiat X1/9, Austin-Healey Sprite, Datsun B210, Saab 99, Mazda RX-3, Alfa Romeo Alfetta, Volkswagen Scirocco, Datsun 510, Datsun 280Z and ZX, MGB, Triumph TR-7, Ford Mustang, Chevrolet Camaro, Corvette, Volkswagen Rabbit, AMC Gremlin and Spirit, Opel Manta, Mazda RX-7, BMW 320i, Buick Skylark, Chevrolet

Production, showroom stock, and formula category cars in SCCA competition.

Monza, Renault LeCar, Volvo 142, Lancia Stratos, and all Porsches and all Ferraris.

The only thing the list proves is that nearly any car in the hands of a good driver will work well, particularly if his mechanic has prepared it properly.

Chapter Two explains how to prepare and modify the car, but before we get into that, let's look at the major auto racing clubs and the racing, rallying, or soloing events they offer. As you begin to understand the way the events are run, and the kinds of cars raced in them, you should be able to make a determination as to the kind of car that would be right for your own racing goals and abilities. Once you've got a car, you should join one of the two organizations available to all, SCCA and IMSA. Here is a fairly detailed account of each:

Sports Car Club of America

Born of a handful of men with a common interest, the Sports Car Club of America, Inc., was founded in Boston on February 26, 1944. A common interest—the love of the automobile—was the primary basis for what has evolved into the most active membership participation organization in the history of motor sports.

Multifaceted in its endeavors, the SCAA might best be described as a service organization. It serves its 20,000-plus members by sanctioning and administering a variety of automotive-related activities through its 100 independently chartered regional clubs.

No other single motor sports organization in the world conducts more events than the SCCA. These vary from SCCA amateur and professional series road races to the internationally listed world championship events; and from the weekend auto rally, hillclimb, and autocross to competition crowning national champions.

As the nation's foremost road racing and rallying sanctioning body, SCCA is a member of the Automobile Competition Committee for the United States (ACCUS). Founded in 1957, ACCUS is recognized by the world motor sports governing body, Federation Internationale de l'Automobile (FIA), as the national club of the United States in all international motor sports affairs. It is through ACCUS–FIA that the SCCA sanctions such premier events as the United States Grand Prix.

With the help and supervision of its member-volunteer force, the SCCA annually conducts more than 1,500 separate events—275-plus are races, and an additional 1,250 nonspeed events are listed on the SCCA calendar —witnessed annually by more than a million fans.

The SCCA now has more than 5,000 specially licensed race drivers— nearly 1,000 members competing in national and professional rally series, and more than double that number in autocross and hillclimb events.

Selecting the Car and the Arena

CRC Trans-Am action. Top: *Mark Pielsticker's Monza (33) outruns a pack of Corvettes.* Middle: *Ray Williams's 1980 Corvette.* Bottom: *James Kersey's Monza leads Bob Leitsinger's Datsun 280ZX.*

Pro Racing

The most widely publicized type of closed-circuit racing the SCCA sanctions are its four major professional series.

The "new era" SCCA Can-Am Challenge, attracting some of the finest road racing drivers in the world, features sleek sports racing cars powered by potent stock block engines and specialized racing engines.

SCCA's longest continuing series, since 1966, is the Trans-AM Championship for popular domestic and foreign touring and grand touring (GT) cars. The series offers two driver championships and three manufacturer crowns. The endless list of marques contending the Trans-Am—Porsche, Camaro, Corvette, Javelin, Cobra, Jaguar, Datsun, Mustang, and more— gives tremendous fan appeal to this type of road racing.

The Robert Bosch Corp./Volkswagen of America sponsors the Gold Cup Series for Formula Super Vee, which has gained instant success with competitors and spectators alike. The fact that all of the cars are powered by a like engine—the 1,600cc VW powerplant—means that success on the circuit is dependent upon the driver's ability. These agile, open-wheel, single-seat racers provide some of the closest competition to be seen in all of motor racing, with victories often decided by less than a second.

Bumper-to-bumper racing, drafting, and squealing tires are all standard style in the Scirocco/Bilstein Cup Pro Series. The VW Scirocco sports car in showroom, street driving trim is the only car eligible for this fiercely competitive racing series.

Club Racing

Although not professional in the traditional sense of the word, the SCCA's National Championship Road Racing Series produces some of the finest competition in U.S. racing.

At least six weekends of races are staged in each of SCCA's seven geographical divisions to determine the best drivers in twenty-four classes of cars. After season-long competition, the top-ranked drivers from throughout the United States are invited to an autumn "Olympics of road racing" to determine national class champions.

From this type of competition have come today's road racing stars, and this is where the stars of tomorrow will gain recognition. The SCCA program of driver training and club racing offers a unique opportunity to gain experience without championship pressure.

Anyone 18 years of age and older who possesses a valid state driver's license and is in top physical condition qualifies for the driver training program. Aspiring drivers must complete at least two SCCA-conducted driving schools, gaining on-track instruction from qualified senior drivers. Once stringent exams and observed competition are completed, a novice driver showing proficiency earns a competition license.

Selecting the Car and the Arena

SCCA club racing has one striking characteristic—variety. Competitors are primarily "weekend warriors" who are employed in shops and offices during the week. Of the forty road racing courses on which they compete, no two are the same. And the automobiles are just as varied.

Any given SCCA regional or national race weekend offers competition in five categories: mass-produced production sports cars in six classes; three classes of domestic and foreign sedans; a wide variety of open-wheel, single-seat formula cars in six classes; four classes of sports racing machines; and three for sports cars and sedans in showroom stock trim.

Solo Events

SCCA competition goes beyond the realm of racing, however, offering a wide range of activities to the automotive enthusiast. One of the most popular races is the solo, where the challenge is "you against the clock."

The SCCA solo events program is divided into two basic categories: Solo I and Solo II. In broad terms, Solo I events are single-car speed competitions calling for safety equipment and organization akin to racing. Solo II events are single-car nonspeed competitions emphasizing driver adeptness and car maneuverability rather than breakneck speed.

Solo I, like Solo II, excludes wheel-to-wheel competition, but the drivers must be licensed for competition and the cars prepared to meet strict safety standards.

The logical step upward toward a racing license, Solo I events are basically of two types: hillclimbs and time trials, where the object is to get the car up the mountain or around the course faster than anyone else.

Solo II is a mushrooming area of activity with more than 900 such events conducted annually by SCCA regional clubs. Top competitors on the divisional level now are eligible to compete for national class titles each autumn at the SCCA National Solo II Championships.

These autocrosses, gymkhanas, slaloms, or field trials are held at parking lots, open fields, airports, and, in the winter, on frozen lakes. Open to anyone with a valid driver's license and an automobile, the many Solo II classes accommodate the full range of domestic and imported cars as well as race-prepared cars. These events offer the enthusiast an opportunity to gauge himself against his peers while becoming more proficient in daily driving.

Rallies

Among the most popular events are rallies—fascinating, demanding, competitive games of navigational skill. The contests range from fun, gimmicky events to SCCA's highly competitive National Club Rally Championship.

In the rally, as in any SCCA competition, all kinds of people of all ages participate. The driver, naturally, must have a valid state driver's license, but the navigator need not be old enough to drive to enjoy the sport. The vehicles are as varied as the drivers—anything with four wheels, properly licensed, and in safe condition will do.

Run on public roads, at or below legal speeds, rallies are scored on the ability of the driver/navigator team to arrive at an unknown control point neither early nor late, but exactly on time. Route instructions are the team's guide; navigational equipment ranges from pencil and paper and the car's odometer to sophisticated electronic computational devices.

SCCA's highest challenge in time-speed-distance (TSD) rally competition is the National Club Rally Championship. This program presents events of considerable challenge and recognition with a separate scoring class for competitors who don't have elaborate computation equipment. This series annually includes some fifty events attracting thousands of rallyists with an eye for a national championship title.

Apart from TSD competition, and rapidly gaining in popularity, is SCCA's National Pro Rally Championship. This annual series of events, an evolution of the well-known Press On Regardless in Michigan, offers the serious rallyist a taste of rugged international competition.

Driver ability and vehicle preparation, both put to extreme tests on roads that are often nothing more than trails, mean the difference between winning and losing a pro rally.

Event Workers

In order to successfully sanction and conduct such a comprehensive program of road racing, solo events, and rallies, a horde of experts in timing, scoring, communications, flagging, safety inspection, and other administrative skills is needed.

The SCCA has such a group of workers, many of them licensed in their specialty and nearly all of them recruited from the club's own membership.

Training is provided through weekend or evening schools, apprentice programs, and on-the-job instruction under licensed experts.

The chief incentive for these volunteers is their desire to participate in the event and the knowledge of a job well done.

Competition Safety

Strong emphasis is placed on safety inspection of all types and classes of cars entering any SCCA competition.

Inspection goes well beyond superficial hazards at races, Solo I events, and pro rallies. Electrical wiring, suspension, firewall, roll bars, safety harnesses, helmets, and fire-resistant uniforms are among the many items scrutinized before a driver is allowed to compete.

Selecting the Car and the Arena

At the nonspeed events—rallies and Solo II—tires, seat belts, brakes, and all light systems are inspected.

Race-circuit safety is also a primary function of SCCA. The forty circuits at which SCCA conducts events are inspected at least every other year. The condition of the racing surface, installation of safety barriers for the protection of participants and spectators, completion of recommended improvements must all be approved before an SCCA sanction is granted. Rally routes and solo courses receive the same close scrutiny.

Organization

The high standard of competition presented by the SCCA, be it racing, rallying, or solo events, lies in the club's unique organizational structure.

The Sports Car Club of America is a nonprofit corporation with headquarters in Denver, where two dozen people are charged with the day-to-day administration of the club's activities.

Chartered by the national organization, the semi-autonomous regions span the fifty states. Each region elects its own volunteer officers, conducts a wide variety of automotive events in its locality, and holds regular social and business meetings. The regions operate independently within the overall national framework and are banded together into divisions for competition purposes, and into areas for elections.

A pack of Can-Am cars prepare to do battle.

The management and general policy for the SCCA is determined by a board of governors, elected by the membership from each of the ten areas. The governors are assisted by specialists named to boards and committees to administer various club affairs and make recommendations to the governing board and national staff.

Because it is member-oriented and member-operated, the SCCA stresses participation on a broad basis. The more than one hundred national and divisional officers and committeemen come from all walks of life and all parts of the country, as do all the members. Their position in the club is based both on their ability to serve the membership and their deep interest in maintaining and improving the organization. This is reflected in the growth of the SCCA to its present size of 20,000-plus members who have found the joy of association with those of a like interest.

Each member of the SCCA holds dual membership—in the national organization and in a region—and regular, spouse, junior, and associate memberships are available. The advantages of SCCA membership are many. In addition to the varied activities, the SCCA has its own monthly magazine, *Sports Car,* and offers several low-cost insurance plans as well as merchandise discount programs.

Here's how to contact SCCA for more information:

Sports Car Club of America, Inc.
National Headquarters
P.O. Box 22476
Denver, Colorado 80222
(303) 751-4900

The International Motor Sports Association

The International Motor Sports Association (IMSA) passed the 300-race mark in 1979 and in 1980 moved into its second decade. Actually, IMSA ran a total of 310 races in 1980 and for the past several years has boasted a stable schedule of events at the major North American tracks in three prosperous and separate series.

IMSA concerns itself strictly with the racing business. Its members are limited to licensed, active participants—race drivers, crew members, industry representatives and officials—and there were a record 2,785 of them in 1979. The organization has a small, professional staff, all of them experts able to run a race anywhere by taking charge of the chief jobs.

IMSA's GT Series was the premier road racing attraction on fifteen weekends in 1980. It is a showcase for international-caliber drivers in some

George Drolsom's Porsche 911 IMSA GTU car.

of the most advanced race car designs with World Championship and World Challenge status for many races. The same series features "races within the race" for two hotly contested separate championships, the GTO Division (Group 4 cars over 2.5 liters displacement) and GTU Division (Group 4 cars under 2.5 liters displacement). For eight years, the R.J. Reynolds Tobacco Company sponsored the GT Series through its Camel Filters and Winston Filters brands.

The Champion Spark Plug Company has supported IMSA racing since the early days of struggle, as it has long supported nearly every form of motor sport. But in a corporate departure two years ago, Champion announced sponsorship of IMSA's popular series for small sedans racing on street radial tires as the Champion Spark Plug Challenge, the RS Series. This remarkable form of racing has prospered since 1971, but the promotional attention of the Champion Spark Plug Company tremendously enhanced its prominence and prestige.

In 1979, IMSA's youngest series, the Kellygirl Challenge, came into being. America's leading temporary-help organization, Kelly Services, Inc., stepped in as a full-fledged backer of these intriguing races for American V-8 and six-cylinder sedans on road courses. The impressive Kellygirl sponsorship quickly brought the series nationwide attention and twenty-car starting fields with tremendous potential for the future as well as a great sports opportunity for women competitors.

IMSA runs a stable schedule of traditional crowd attractions at nearly every major road course in the United States and Canada. New, major successes were added at Riverside, California, Road America in Wisconsin, and Mosport Park in Canada. IMSA continues to "race with a difference" while serving competitors with a program of prestige and the racing industry with an invaluable marketing platform. IMSA welcomes active members, including corporate members. More information is available from:

Playboy's Guide to . . . Sports Car Driving

International Motor Sports Association
P.O. Box 3465
Bridgeport, Connecticut 06605
(203) 336-2116

RS Series

RS (racing stock) is limited to compacts and subcompacts, with roll cages and street radial tires. It is one of the most controlled forms of racing and, consequently, one of the least expensive to the competitors. It began in 1970 and has since become so popular that it is now referred to as the world's only successful example of handicap racing.

It works in a wondrous and arcane manner, but the facts are straightforward. Chassis stress is limited and expensive suspension modifications are eliminated by requiring Goodyear Wingfoot or Goodrich Radial T/A tires. Carburetion is restricted in ways that make most high-performance engine components pointless. Playing with the required minimum weights lets IMSA claim and prove that 1,400cc Renaults can run alongside 3,800cc Spirits.

It works so well that 72 starting cars in six races the inaugural season rocketed to 900 starting cars in fifteen races within five years. Battling for position throughout the field is a hallmark of RS racing. Battling for the lead is another one, as demonstrated by 1979's nine different winners in six different makes of cars in sixteen races.

GT Racing

In 1971 the young IMSA organization did a simple and obvious thing that nobody had thought of doing earlier: President John Bishop mixed together the then popular pony cars and high-performance sports cars. Previously, each had been in its own niche of racing. He called the mixture Grand Touring (GT), and fans quickly showed they liked watching Cama-

Roger Mandeville's Mazda RX-3 IMSA championship-winning RS car.

The Bob Tullius Triumph TR-8 IMSA GTO car.

ros, Javelins, Mustangs, and Challengers dice with Porsches, Corvettes, Panteras, and Lotuses.

Many new cars have appeared since then. There have been new models from the classic GT car makers, and many entirely new nameplates have become prominent GT competitors—BMW, Datsun, Ferrari, Monza, Mazda, Triumph.

The public has been the real winner of the GT concept, especially with IMSA's invention of the racing Monza. While the special All-American GT rules for cars like the IMSA Monza do not stray far from the internationally recognized FIA regulations, this is a candid attempt to help American race shops compete with the kind of high-performance cars the European racing factories have been building for years. Successful? The Monza has twice been the chosen car of the series champion.

It's a bit hard to believe, but the 1970s wound up as a decade that will go into the books as the "GT era." Little blocks of years in the '60s and even the '50s had their favorite racing classes and cars that were briefly "in style." In retrospect, they were Roman candles, fuel for nostalgia—brightly up, then down and out.

But "GT racing"—not even a definable term in 1970—was an immediate success when IMSA invented it and, ten years later, it was dominating the American road racing scene. Car makers everywhere chrome-plate the letters to quarter-panels, and rubber companies emboss GT on sidewalls.

They used to have to explain, "It stands for Grand Touring or Gran Turismo, and it's both a type of car and a concept of driving. . . ." But today, GT racing is the big event at nearly every major road course in the country and the term "GT" is in everyone's vocabulary.

Wheel to Wheel

Perhaps everything has already begun to run together—road racing, rallying, solo, GT, RS. Basically, there are five different categories of car in road racing: formula, sports racing, production, showroom stock, and GT.

In SCCA racing there are two groups roughly derived from street-type cars. One group includes the production and GT cars, sports cars in one category and sedans in another. Some day soon they will probably be combined into a GT category on the theory that eventually there won't be any more rag top cars. There are classes within the production category, and they are classified by performance potential—that is, the faster cars, regardless of displacement or suspension will be the faster classes and so on down to the cars like Sprites, which are the slowest.

The other broad group of cars includes the pure racing cars, which are largely related in one way or another—directly or remotely—to international racing classes. Categories in this group are formula and sports racing. Formula cars are single-seaters, open-wheeled, generally with a rather strict formula for their displacement and other rules of construction. Sports racing cars are more loosely related to production cars or the prototype production cars of the future—that's the way they got their start—so they generally have two seats and full fenders, with very little in the way of restriction beyond that. Both categories are classified not by performance potential, but by the size of their engines.

The showroom stock category mandates that the cars are to be raced as they are delivered from the factory. Oddly enough, some of the wildest competition in SCCA is in this category.

The following are the specifications for the SCAA categories:

Category: Formula—Pure racing cars, open-wheel (no fenders), single-seat machines similar to Indy and Formula One cars.

Fred Baker's showroom stock Porsche 924.

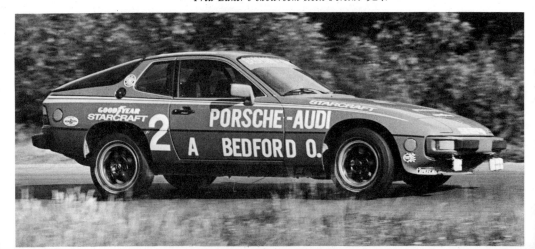

Selecting the Car and the Arena

Classes: Atlantic. Modified 1,600cc (98ci), production-based engine.

Ford. 1,600cc Ford Cortina/Fiesta/Pinto engines only, with limited modifications.

Vee. Based on 1,200cc VW components, VW steering, gearbox, suspension, and wheels.

Continental. Based on VW 1,600cc engines and modified 1,100cc engines.

Category: GT (Grand Touring)—Mass-produced sports sedans with rear-seat passenger carrying capacity, recognized by SCCA. Cars ranging from the Honda Civic to Fiat 124, and Datsun 710 to the Ford Mustang, Corvette, and Ferrari race in these four classes. Performance within a class is equalized by keying car weight to engine displacement so that cars with smaller engines compete at a lighter weight.

Classes: GT-1   Over 2,500cc
          GT-2   1,800–2,000cc
          GT-3   1,400–1,600cc
          GT-4   Up to 1,300cc

Category: Production—Mass-produced sports cars ranging from Datsun Z, Porsche, Mazda RX-7, and Triumph TR8 to MG Midget and Austin-Healey Sprite. These cars resemble street cars, but are permitted extensive race modifications in the interest of increased performance. Cars are classified by performance potential, not engine size. This offers more and better racing for a larger variety of models, including many that are no longer in production.

Classes: C, D, E, F, G, and H in descending order of performance potential based on displacement, car weight, and handling.

Category: Sports Racing—Sports cars that are nearly unlimited in design, which compete according to engine size. They have two seats and four fenders, but are very stark in fittings. They are also known as FIA Group 7 cars and range from the V-8 powered McLarens and Lolas to a one-of-a-kind home-built special with motorcycle engines. They offer probably the best opportunity in racing for individual ingenuity in auto design.

Classes: A   1,300cc–5,000cc
          C   850cc–1,300cc
          D   Up to 850cc
          Sports   2,000 (2,000cc)

Category: Showroom Stock—These mass-produced sports cars are raced just as they are sold from the showroom floor. No modification is allowed except for the addition of driver safety equipment. They must all be no more than three years old.

Classes: A, B, and C in descending order of performance.

For a listing of the specific cars included in each class, see Appendix.

Part of the fascination for the SCCA beginning racer is that there is no *obvious* starting category. There's a space for almost everyone, a place where drivers can exercise their technical talent and where they can spend money if they have it. Or, it offers in showroom stock, a category where they can go racing at a relatively low cost with little technical involvement.

If you would like to develop a car and work on it a lot, there are all sorts of opportunities for you to do just that. A production or GT car, for example, is an incredibly involved, intricate, and expensive device. If you wanted Bob Sharp to build you one of his racing Datsun 280 ZXs, it would probably cost you in the neighborhood of $40,000, less engine. That's how intricate and expensive *competitive* cars are in certain categories. Although you can simply buy all that (and a lot of people are capable of doing so), you might instead decide to buy the parts and the car and put it all together yourself. Either way, it won't be cheap.

So, for starters, you have to pick the sort of thing that pleases you most: Do you like to twist a wrench? Or would you rather go to the races and step into a car that's already been prepared for you, with no need to get your own hands dirty? And what is your level of driving skill?

No one who has just gotten a first driver's license for the highway should attempt to go straight to the race track. You must have an ample amount of driving experience, or an awful lot of natural ability. Judgment and technique are way ahead of bravery.

But, once you've satisfied yourself that you can handle an automobile on the highway in a safe and sane manner, have enough experience not to panic in an emergency, and feel comfortable in any highway situation—not white-knuckled, comfortable—then you can start investigating road racing. The level of competency in club racing is such that you won't get in over your head, regardless of the car you are in; unless, of course, you pick Formula Atlantic or a car that has incredible potential. Even then, you could probably do it, but it would be foolish because you would just be at the back of the pack and in everybody else's way. But, if you've got any head on your shoulders at all, you probably won't get in over it.

Winning is something else. It depends upon how well you prepare your car, how much you spend, and how well you prepare yourself. It may sound repetitious, and it is, but good preparation is still the basic *law.*

Sometimes money can actually get in the way. There are people who have gone out and bought a formula car to start with and found themselves in completely the wrong place. They didn't necessarily get into trouble, but they would have been much better off had they started in, say, a production category first, and first mastered that. There is fierce competition in this category, but it is not one in which only the seasoned veterans have a chance.

Elliott Forbes-Robinson said of Formula Atlantic cars, for example,

Patrick Tanbay in Carl Haas's Lola T-530 Can-Am car.

"They do everything well. They corner well, they accelerate well, everything." Obviously, then, to drive them to the limit of their capability, you have to be able to drive very, very fast. It takes some real technique. So, even if you don't get in over your head, you could miss the actual thrill of racing. Oh, there might be some thrill there, but not the thrill of true racing competition—the wheel-to-wheel, nose-to-tail adrenalin-pumping thrill of racing. You might be better off on that back stretch of highway.

In one of the advanced categories, you could *discourage* yourself rather than actually hurt yourself, although the latter certainly isn't out of the realm of possibility. It remains a question of perspective whether or not you get the true feel of racing out of a sedan as compared to a sports racing car or a formula car. Once you've driven them all, you can tell the incredible difference.

Until you have actually driven a car that was designed and built for racing, you simply won't be able to appreciate what a race car can do in terms of braking, cornering, and accelerating. There just isn't any way to understand that, certainly not in any GT car we have now. Even the Bob Sharp Z cars, as fantastically well prepared as they are, just don't have it, compared to a little sports racer. Some of the sports racers can go around a tight course a couple of seconds faster, and they can do it with, say, 750cc. Compare this with the 280-horsepower of the Z that maybe can hit 150 miles per hour at the end of the straight and it's hard to imagine, but the sports racers and formula cars just handle that much better. A real race car gives you the sensation of the capability of a car a whole lot better than a sedan. But there is still plenty of fun and first-rate competition in production or showroom stock racing.

Before you run out and buy a car, it might be wise to get to know some people in racing. Go to a few races and see what's going on, which cars are doing well, what looks exciting to you, and, most importantly, what you can afford. Then consider what you think you might be able to handle in terms of speed and technical involvement. It is a different level for each person, so, again, there is no one answer.

Assuming that you are interested in a car that is derived from a production car, a little sedan or a roadster, you would probably look at a Datsun product or a Jaguar-Rover-Triumph (J-R-T) car or perhaps a Mazda RX-7 or Fiat X1/9. There is a lot to choose from, and the earlier list of winning cars might help.

If you are really interested in mechanics, you might look around for an older car, one out of production, the Sprite, for example. The Sprite hasn't even been produced for nearly twenty years, but it's still the winningest car in H Production class, as is the old bathtub Porsche (356) in E Production. But you really have to dig for them, and you have to be capable of preparing them. You may even find one that is already prepared—but be ready to pay a healthy price for it. Most people aren't ready to do that, however, so they buy a Datsun or a J-R-T or a Fiat and then get a lot of information from the manufacturer on how to prepare the car for racing. In fact, from most of the companies you can get a book that tells you step by step what to do. And, if you do all the things they tell you to do, you will go to your first race with a car that is very capable.

You might prepare a Datsun 280ZX for C Production or a Datsun 510 for GT3 or a Triumph TR-8 for C Production. Or you can get a 924 Porsche for D Production, but this is an expensive car. Porsche will sell you a whole car, starting with a body shell (which is called a body in white) and all the components you need to build a car from the ground up—a complete

A 1953 Triumph TR-2, one of many race drivers' first cars. The Triumph is still a favorite SCCA racer.

The Austin-Healey 100 was for years one of the most successful race cars and highway machines imported into the United States. It took little to get it track-ready.

suspension, roll cage, everything. Datsun will do the same thing; J-R-T doesn't sell the parts over the counter, but they will tell you where to get them and *what* to get. But, whatever you do, buy race-prepared parts. They will stand up much longer in competition.

If you take the easier, if more expensive, route and buy a used race car, buy a winner, one that is at least *capable* of winning. Obviously, some of the bugs will already have been ironed out of that particular car and most of the problems will have been solved. But, as with many used cars, you won't know exactly what you are getting. Even if you were to buy a leftover Roger Penske car, with all the perfection of maintenance and operation it would have, you still wouldn't know when an axle was likely to break or some other part might let go in the middle of the hairpin. A lot of people do go the used race car route, however, and, if you can find the right car, you can get into racing a little cheaper and with a lot less effort, particularly if you find a car owned by someone who is moving up to another class or getting out of racing completely. In either case, you might be able to find one that is not completely used up.

If, on the other hand, you find a car that is owned by someone who is simply buying or building another car of the same type and class, you can assume that he has gotten everything possible out of the old car, otherwise he would still be racing it himself. *It is always cheaper to repair than to build new.* It is a rare case when the repairs are as great as total replacement of the car. It is just like buying a used street car as compared to a new one.

Many times it is cheaper to replace the broken axle or fix half a dozen minor problems as they happen than to go through the time and expense of building from scratch. But, if you buy a used race car, ideally you should take it apart completely and examine the parts. You should even go so far as to have the axles and suspension parts magnafluxed or X-rayed to detect hairline cracks.

People who pay attention to detail even take new engines apart, down to the last bolt, then reassemble them, just to make sure they are absolutely right. They do the same with suspensions and rear ends. It's not that they get their kicks from taking things apart; it's just that they want to be sure they are at least *starting* with everything as perfect as possible. It is not surprising that they are usually the ones still running at the finish of a race. Unfortunately, not too many people have the time or money—or perhaps the persistence or personality—to take a car apart down to the last bolt. It usually doesn't happen, so if you are not prepared to go that far, you might be better off starting from scratch.

Aside from the expense, a broken part in a race means (1) you have lost the race, and (2) you might seriously damage the sheet metal or yourself. Racing is not a cheap sport. And the faster you go, the more it is going to cost. When you go very fast, for instance, you may use up a new set of tires every weekend. Because of the soft compound used on high-speed racing tires—the sticky ones—they don't last long. After one hard use or race, they will have heated up to the point that they actually cure themselves, and then they begin to lose some of their original adhesion. So you will find yourself using them for practice and qualifying the following weekend and putting on a new set of rubber for the race. It gets very expensive as you get closer to that last mile per hour.

Some people in showroom stock drive their cars to work and to the race

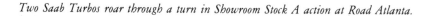

Two Saab Turbos roar through a turn in Showroom Stock A action at Road Atlanta.

track, but, again unfortunately for the wallet, the level of preparation for a winning car in that class is equivalent to the level of competition in the driving itself. So not many of the really successful showroom stock cars ever touch the road, except when they are on the race course. They go to the race on a trailer.

In a sense, the argument about which is the most expensive category—a very much restricted to a preparation rules class like showroom stock or a completely free and open preparation rules class—is one that can't be resolved. On the one hand, people say well, if *anything* goes, it means that you can spend all the money in the world and buy the very best of everything, regardless of its sophistication or expense, and that's true. But, on the other hand, if theoretically you do nothing that the manufacturer didn't do when he built the car, it must be absolute stock to the manufacturer's complete specifications and within his tolerances. There lies the secret: It means the things you *can* do are all listed by the manufacturer's tolerances, but one degree of tolerance or another is certainly going to be the fastest way. So the sophistication to go from bearing clearances of .0025 to bearing clearances of .0030 doesn't give you much to work with, and that is expensive territory. This kind of modification can become considerably more expensive, because the advantage you achieve from all these tiny changes is very small and it takes *a lot* of them to accomplish anything at all. It adds up very quickly, so a showroom stock could conceivably be the most expensive car on the track, if it were prepared to its very ultimate specs. The more competitive the demands, the more these subtle changes are made.

Is this cheating? Not really. If you took, say, twelve identical factory cars, one would be faster; one would have a better combination of clearances and tolerances. But, by the same token, one might last longer. So you really have to *build* that speed and dependability into the showroom stock car.

Formula Vee is one of the most restricted classes of all. It was designed that way to keep costs down, but a few years ago some bright guy found out that a certain type of cylinder wall finish would give him about 2 horsepower more than the rest of the pack had. Well, 2 horsepower out of 50 is a bunch, so when the secret got out—and it always does around a race track; they just can't resist bragging to someone—everybody had to have that finish to remain competitive. That's a fairly sophisticated improvement that obviously wasn't considered by the guys who dreamed up the class, and yet a driver has to be able to repair an engine, and that often means refinishing the cylinder walls, right? The whole thing is typical of the level of sophistication that people in racing must live with.

The problem, of course, is that the average guy who starts racing (1) doesn't have all these little advantages, or (2) doesn't even know he needs them. He usually can't figure out why he's getting outrun so badly and so often. Unless, of course, he's an A.J. Foyt or a Stroker Ace, and there aren't

Nighttime pit action on Dick Barbour's Porsche 935 at Sebring.

many of that caliber around, ones who can take almost anything and be competitive. But there are some people who, right from the beginning, shine a whole lot brighter than others; maybe they're just natural competitors and would win at skiing or surfing or Parcheesi or whatever. They are—if you'll pardon the trite movie-magazine expression—the young, devil-may-care people. The winners.

Drivers like Gilles Villeneuve and Jody Scheckter were considered wild kids when they started. They certainly were going to kill themselves and half the spectators. But they didn't kill themselves, they ended up in Formula One. But this book isn't for the one in a million, it's for the million; those are the ones who go into high-performance driving for a good time, knowing that there is a lot of talent and preparation and capability required. You must realize that you can't simply run in and start winning right away. Even Foyt didn't do that. He got his nose bloodied a lot of times. And Roger Penske took a while to start winning, although when he did his tremendously successful SCCA club racing, his forte was thinking about it better than anybody else and preparing better, coming up with the Mark Donahue type of "Unfair Advantage" because he thought about it harder and worked at it harder.

Selecting the Car and the Arena

What Does It Cost?

The cost of racing obviously varies greatly, depending upon which class you choose, how much of the work you do yourself, and whether or not you buy a race car or build one, new or used. We will take a look at some "middle-level" classes. The figures are merely representative and do not include tools or major shop equipment. They also do not include any sponsorship or contingency money, which, if you are fortunate enough to get, will bring the cost down.

But keep this in mind: As one driver put it, "You pay with dollars or you pay with time. But you pay."

The figures on page 32 were actual ones submitted by SCCA drivers

Rabbit/Bilstein Cup
Volkswagen Rabbit

One of the most interesting classes for beginning drivers is a special one SCCA came up with a few years ago, the Rabbit/Bilstein Cup. It means just that, Volkswagen Rabbits, race-prepared, and run in a series sponsored by Bilstein shocks.

On page 33 is an item-by-item breakdown of the cost of buying and preparing a Rabbit to full race-ready status, listing the precise tools needed. The preparation of this particular Rabbit was typical of that necessary to race in the SCCA series. Because of the high resale value of used Rabbits, there would have been little difference in the final price whether the car had been used or new. This happened to be a new one, purchased in California.

The Decision

It becomes painfully obvious to most that the wallet and one's location often are the determining factors as to what and where one is to race. It would be marvelous if we all could hop into a spanking new Turbo Carrera and go racing—assuming we had the ability to keep it on the course at competitive speeds—and it would be equally gratifying if we could throw a bucket of chicken into the sports racer and drive a mile or so down the road to Lime Rock and race every weekend. Seldom, however, do either of these conditions exist.

Most race drivers begin racing with what is available to them and race wherever they can, which in the long run is probably just as well. It really doesn't matter which car you choose, so long as you are capable of handling

D Sports Racing
Ocelot chassis/Suzuki engine

Rolling chassis (less gearbox)	$14,000
Racing engine	3,150
Gearbox	(integral w/engine)
Tires[1]	856
Entry fees/track rental	602
Parts/spares	3,411
Crash expenses	811
Tow van	4,988
Trailer	716
Travel (gasoline and accommodations)	1,997
Salaries[2]/preparation/shop space rental	2,059
TOTAL COST	32,660
End-of-season resale value	20,570
NET COST	12,090
Per-race average cost (8 races including CSPRRC)	1,511

[1]Used 16 tires; bought 12.
[2]Did most work himself; figure is for Union Jack Racing Shop space rental.

Showroom Stock B
Saab 99 GL

Rolling chassis (less gearbox)	$ 6,189
Racing engine	NA
Gearbox	NA
Tires[3]	1,717
Entry fees/track rental	655
Parts/spares	1,725
Crash expenses	583
Tow van[4]	199
Trailer	NA
Travel (gasoline and accommodations)	978
Salaries[5]/preparation/shop space rental	1,055
TOTAL COST	13,101
End-of-season resale value	5,860
NET COST	7,241
Per-race average cost (10 races)	724

[3]Used 34 tires. Total includes cost of shaving and balancing.
[4]Drove his racer to each event—figure is the cost of street insurance.
[5]Paid mechanic to prepare car between races. Did not have a trackside mechanic.

Formula Vee

Rolling chassis (less gearbox)	$3,453
Racing engine[6]	827
Gearbox[7]	100
Tires[8]	835
Entry fees/track rental	560
Parts/spares	350
Crash expenses	424
Tow van	1,300
Trailer	150
Travel (gasoline and accommodations)	225
Salaries/preparation[9]/shop space rental	NA
TOTAL COST	8,224
End-of-season resale value	4,950
NET COST	3,274
Per-race average cost (8 races including drivers' school)	409

[6&7]Bought an elderly VW for $100 and salvaged most of the parts. Modified his own cylinder heads, as opposed to buying them, the current fashion.
[8]Bought two new sets of tires and two used sets.
[9]Did all own work.

E Production
MGB

Rolling chassis (less gearbox)	$ 4,200
Racing engine	4,500
Gearbox	1,400
Tires[10]	1,400
Entry fees/track rental	300
Parts/spares[11]	8,200
Crash expenses	800
Tow van[12]	NA
Trailer	3,500
Travel (gasoline and accommodations)	2,200
Salaries/preparation/shop space rental	3,000
TOTAL COST	29,500
End-of-season resale value	16,500
NET COST	13,000
Per-race average cost (7 races)	1,857

[10]Used 20 tires.
[11]Includes spare engine and gearbox.
[12]Used van from his business when necessary.

A group of Rabbits in the Rabbit/Bilstein Cup Series.

1980 Rabbit 2-dr. custom	$5,475.00
California emission controls	85.00
Factory options and destination charges	812.00
Dealer options and preparation charges	769.00
TOTAL CAR COST	7,141.00
Bilstein P30 032 front cartridge inserts	178.00/pr.
Bilstein R79 flanging ring kit (for front)	12.00/pr. exchange
Bilstein B46 834 rear shock absorbers	158.00/pr
Bilstein special B46 366R spring perch kit (rear)	N/C exchange
Goodyear 205/60 R13 Wingfoot radials (shaved)	172.68/set of 4 incl. FET[13]
Volkswagen #321 601 025A 5J×13 Dasher road wheels	157.20/set of 4
High-speed wheel balancing	20.00/set of 4
Hacker Racing upper and lower frame stay bars	86.00/pr
Front end alignment	30.00
TOTAL CHASSIS/SUSPENSION	813.88
Autopower SCCA-approved roll bar	149.95
Simpson #29000 3″ lap belt	46.03
Simpson #30005 2″ shoulder harness (request extra 6″)	32.96

[13]Goodyear prices subject to change. Full-tread (rain) tires are available at this price only to recognized racers.

Simpson #31012 antisub belt (with nonslip spring)	10.35
Simpson #31504 18" × 24" window net	16.69
Race Ware (General) 2½ lb. 10BC-rated extinguisher	16.95
VDO Cockpit #333 041 transistorized tachometer	65.50
VDO Cockpit #350 009 oil pressure gauge	40.75
VDO Cockpit #310 007 water temperature gauge	40.75
Hi-back racing seat	325.00
TOTAL INTERIOR EQUIPMENT COST	744.93
Bosch W215 T30 spark plugs	7.28/set of 4[14]
Custom straight pipe (parts and labor)	61.80
Hacker Racing baffled oil pan	90.00/exchange
Volkswagen #056 103 609A oil pan gasket	6.90
Valvoline 20–50 racing oil	4.62/4 quarts[15]
Adjust CO mixture	warranty
Adjust valves	warranty
TOTAL ENGINE COST	170.60
American Autodynamics stripe kits	120.00
3M Co. ScotchCal (for numbers)	14.00
Miscellaneous parts	48.15
MISCELLANEOUS COSTS	182.15
TOTAL COST OF PROJECT CAR	9,052.56

Basic Tools Needed

Set of metric sockets (including deep) 10–19mm
⅜-drive ratchet
Spark plug socket
Set of metric combination wrenches (box and open-end)
Set of screwdrivers (blade and Phillips)
Pliers
Needle-nose pliers
Electrical crimpers/wire cutters
Large hammer
Electric drill
5/16" drill bit
Torque wrench
Accurate tire pressure gauge
"Spike tool"
¼-drive 10mm flex socket
¼-drive 6" extension
¼-drive ratchet
6" steel rule
Small center punch

---

[14]Bosch Corp. services all the Bilstein events, with plugs, rotor distributor caps, and new oil filter product for racers.

[15]Valvoline supports the series with product and technical reps.

Selecting the Car and the Arena

Special Tools Needed

Spring compressor, front strut
7mm Allen wrench or socket, front strut
22mm S-shaped box wrench, front strut
Spring-platform tool, front strut
30mm ½-drive socket, front hub nut
200-lb. torque wrench, front hub nut
Star-headed 10mm socket, cylinder head
Valve adjustment special tool, valve adjustment
Assortment of valve shims (2.9 to 4.0), valve adjustment
Camber gauge, alignment
Toe-in optical gauges, alignment
24 mm ½-drive socket, alignment (steering wheel adjust)
CO meter, mixture
3 mm long Allen key, mixture
Welding equipment, exhaust
Exhaust pipe bender, exhaust

Miscellaneous Before You Start

Assortment of ty-wraps (6″ and 12″)
1-quart plastic (or other) container (catch can)
¾″ heater nose (3′) for breather
Air-tight rubber plug (for air cleaner fitting)
Assortment of hose clamps (breather, fire extinguisher)
1¾″ exhaust pipe (5′ for side outlet)
Catalytic converter flange (cut off old or from dealer junk)
Flexible muffler hanger
Safety wire
Silicone (or other) seal (to waterproof holes in floor)
Electrical connectors (for gauges)
Electrical tape
Racer's tape
Razor
Extra WV #321 881 213C nylon guards

it and it is well prepared. There will be ample time to move up in class or category once you have mastered the basics. And there will be arenas in which to compete, no matter what stage of development you reach.

As your skill and equipment improve, so, too, will your desire and ability to tow the machine to distant places if necessary in search of gold. So this brings us to another important rule. Important Rule: Don't go too fast *too soon.*

2

To Build or Not to Build

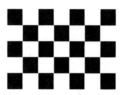

To give the proper perspective as to which car you might buy and how you can improve it, here's a brief description of what the Sports Car Club of America allows you to do:

The production category is comprised of sports cars which generally are available to the public in quantities of at least 1,000 each year. Slight body modifications are allowed, racing tires can be fitted, and certain replacements and improvements can be made to shocks, brakes, electrical system, carburetion, suspension, and engine. In short, the cars may be modified within SCCA limitations to make them faster, better handling, and cosmetically more race-like. Specific changes in this and all SCCA categories are covered in detail in literature available from the organization.

The GT category is much the same as production except that 5,000 cars in the specific class must be produced each year. They are what we generally consider to be sports sedans—grand touring cars.

The sports racing category is intended for automobiles that are designed and constructed specifically for road racing, with one or two seats. These are true race cars, so there are far fewer restrictions on them than on production cars. Classes are determined, as in all categories, by performance potential.

Formula cars are single seat, four open-wheel racing cars. Like sports racing cars, they are true race cars and are relatively unrestricted when compared to production or GT cars.

To Build or Not to Build

Showroom stock stands for precisely what the name implies. These are street stock cars and must remain in "as delivered" condition with only safety equipment (belts, roll bars, fire extinguishers) added. Simple.

The degree to which you prepare a car depends entirely upon how you intend to use it once it's been modified. Obviously, you wouldn't modify a car for rallying in the same way you would for an SCCA race. And, odd as it might sound, preparation depends on how many cars you have. By that I mean you can't go all-out modifying a car if you have to drive it to work on Monday morning. But, if you own a second car and a trailer, you can go as far as your conscience or your bank account will allow.

The woebegone bank account, unfortunately, again comes into focus when you look at the economy factor, because few modifications actually improve the economy of a vehicle. For example, the improved mileage resulting from the use of headers or from changing a two-barrel carburetor to a four-barrel one is often neutralized by what you are likely to do with the long pedal on the floorboard once you get the extra horses. There is not one of us in a thousand who can resist pushing it a little harder when we know we have that extra power under the hood. And the mile, or fraction

The Porsche Turbo Carrera (at bottom) has been one of the most successful highway/racing cars ever produced, and the 911 (top) has been tough to beat in racing, solo, or rallying.

thereof, per gallon you may gain goes right down the four-barrel when you nail it.

You can, however, rationalize it this way: Many of the very basic improvements required to make a car handle even better—whether it's a Buick or a Porsche—are common to all forms of automotive competition. And they really should be made even if you intend only to drive spiritedly on the street, the arena where most of us end up.

The two people I consulted on how-to-and-what-to come complete with an impressive set of credentials. Bob Sharp was a champion driver many times before he turned from a Lecarra steering wheel to a Crescent wrench. In fact, he won every IMSA race he entered in his final season—a most dramatic time to quit. But a record like his is as much a tribute to race car preparation and maintenance as it is to driving skill. To win every race— or even some of them—you have to do everything right in the first place, and check very, very often to make sure it all remains right. You simply can't leave anything to chance.

Following Sharp's retirement from chauffeuring race cars, he began building them, and today his racing Datsuns are considered by many to be the standard of excellence in both SCCA and IMSA national events. Many pitside conversations begin with the words, "Well, Sharp does it this way. . . ."

On the highway side of automobile modification, Bill Mitchell is the man consulted by most informed car enthusiasts—auto manufacturers and tinkerers alike. Mitchell has done more to boost (if you'll pardon the expression) the art of turbocharging street machines than any man alive. He has turboed everything from Corvettes to Chevettes. His Connecticut shop is a familiar spot not just for speed freaks but for the person who just wants his car to perform the way a stock machine did in the '50s or '60s. Oddly, many of his customers are traveling salesmen who are forced to spend vast amounts of time in the confines of their cars. Even corporate executives send their company cars to Mitchell for "improvements." And, just as often, the cars come away more economical as well as more powerful.

Bob Sharp and Bill Mitchell are tops in their fields. So it was hardly surprising that their comments and suggestions were amazingly similar, whether they were talking about street or track.

"To get ready to race," says Sharp, "it is critical as to what kind of car you're talking about. Datsuns, for instance, are very neutral handling cars, so it's relatively easy to take one and go showroom stock racing. You put in a roll bar, belts, and shoulder harness, fire extinguisher, tape up the headlights, and you go racing. Granted, with stock tires—even shaved-down stock tires—it's not going to be the best race car in the world, but it's going to be very comfortable for the average beginner."

"Comfortable" is the key word in Sharp's opening remark about racing.

38

Don Devendorf's Datsun 280ZX IMSA GTU car.

Nobody should ever get so far ahead of his ability that he is *un*comfortable. That is the very reason Bob Bondurant uses Datsuns in his driving school. They are neutral and controllable. Comfortable, if you please.

When you get into some cars, like the front-engined Volkswagen Rabbit or the rear-engined Porsche 911, you have a car with very different characteristics. So it is difficult to generalize. You can't just say, "Do this" and find that your advice works for every car. Some require a lot to make them handle well, or even acceptably.

The only way a neophyte can gain any confidence is with a car that is very controllable. You can take a Datsun Z or a sedan to driving school or Lime Rock and build up your confidence level. When you say to someone, "You'll be able to drive through this turn or that turn at, say, ninety miles an hour," it sounds very fast. But after half an hour of not worrying about kids and dogs and telephone poles and stone walls and all the things that build up subliminal pressure on your brain when you're driving to the grocery store, you can work up to 90 miles an hour very quickly, and it's not at all scary.

You can learn in showroom stock, for instance, that by pumping the brakes a few times to get some air in there you don't overheat them as much. And, since most road cars aren't equipped with air ducts for the brakes, you want to do everything you can to keep them relatively cool.

You must eliminate as many worries as possible in the beginning. If you don't have to fight overheated brakes or oversteer or understeer, you will be free to concentrate on some of the other things that can be awe-inspiring to a new driver. People like Sharp have learned through experience that if

39

you have to spend time worrying about the car, you'll never get to the winner's circle. They know that all parts that are to be stressed must be magnafluxed (X-rayed) before racing—wheels, axles, and suspension parts, as well as engine parts. You can't wait until something breaks and then fix it, because, for one thing, it will probably break at a very inopportune time, like in the middle of a turn—a dismal experience. Everything about the car has to be as strong and fresh as possible going in. A lot more races are won by building the car right in the winter time than they are by trying to scramble around and get things fixed on a race weekend.

"Racing can be an extremely expensive sport," says Sharp. "I've had hundreds of young fellows aspiring to be race drivers over the years, and I usually try to start them out in showroom stock. At least they can get the feel of it. They can start out completely stock and find out if they've bitten off more than they can chew. And if they find out that they're not interested in taking it that seriously by going the next several steps it takes to become a winner, they can return the car to normal, sell the roll bar and shoulder harness and go fishing.

"But about fifty percent of the people I talk to want something more competitive right off. They're not willing to go showroom stock. I suppose a lot of them already have sway bars and spoilers and good shocks on their street machines and they've seen how much it has improved their road car, so they're not too enthusiastic about taking a boxy stock sedan where they can't even make *those* changes and go racing. They consider it to be a 'sub-road car.' "

What about these people who *know* they want to go racing—perhaps the ones who have done some solo driving and have spent a few bucks over the years on their cars, and who have a little money to spend?

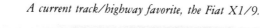

A current track/highway favorite, the Fiat X1/9.

If racing or street machine funds were unlimited, most enthusiasts would be driving a high-performance machine like the ones pictured here: Ferrari (top), Lotus Esprit (middle), or BMW (bottom). Unfortunately, most are faced with trying to make their machines go and handle like a Ferrari, Lotus, or BMW.

"What the majority of them do," according to Sharp, "is, they buy a half-clapped-out race car—because it's cheap—something like a Datsun 510 sedan with an engine that's about to explode and a transmission that's three-fourths worn out and a squealing rear end, and brakes that weren't right to begin with, and they start going through the car at two thousand dollars a pop. And twelve thousand dollars later it's still not a fully prepared race car.

"The guy who really wants to do it right is far better off to buy the very best race car he can find, assuming, of course, that he doesn't want to do the work himself, or he doesn't have the time or space. But if he buys a year-old team car from people like us or Bob Tullins, he'll know what he's getting. When they're ready to sell a car, you can figure that the car is in tip-top condition, because nobody is going to put a top driver in a car that has anything marginal in it."

Starting out in a car that is in top condition, one that has a maintenance history, you will probably be way ahead of the game. For one thing, you can look at the maintenance records and tell how often you should throw something away and replace it. Valuable information that is hard to come by. Since 90 percent of the people don't race that way, you've got an advantage over them from the start. Most do it as they wander along, which is exactly why 90 percent of them never win.

As in almost any other form of competition, it takes total dedication to win. That means taking your car very seriously, and, in many cases, spending upwards of $50,000 to *build* the car. The guy who buys the half-clapped-out race car and tries to upgrade it into a beautiful racer is going to wind up dribbling in as much money in the long run—as well as an awful lot of time and frustration along the way—and he's not going to finish a lot of races. It is tough to stand up and bite the bullet at the beginning; it's a lot easier to dump a couple of grand into the car every month or so. It's impossible for many to walk up to the counter and write a check for $30,000 for a used race car, but it's the only way to buy a certified winner.

"Most reputable teams, when selling a car, will agree to come to the first test session, and that's important," says Sharp. "The guy who is used to the car can take it out and drive it, and he can be sure it's right. Then they can put the neophyte in the car and know, from the beginning, he is going to have a car that is set up properly."

Even some of the cars used by driving schools may have three or four problems, which the new driver isn't even sophisticated enough to detect. He doesn't know what a really well-prepared car is like. He may be in a car that's understeering like crazy and think that *all* Triumphs handle that way. It's the nature of a driving school operation; a car that's been driven by a hundred guys is a lot different than one that's been driven by just one person.

To Build or Not to Build

Let's assume you've been through driving school, and after a few show-room stock races the bug really bites you. You want to buy a production car, F or E—a Triumph or an MGB or a sedan of some kind—one that has enough power to make it interesting, maybe 120 miles an hour: a good, safe, stable, solid car. Well, unless you're being tutored by a pretty professional MGB driver, it's going to take you a long time to figure out how the car ought to feel. When you come up against a similar kind of car that beats you because it's handling better, you'll go home scratching your head, saying, "You know, I don't think my car's handling right. I couldn't stay with that guy, and my line was as good as his, but he made it through the corner faster than I did. . . ."

Now where do you go? What do you do to remedy the problem? There aren't a lot of shops around that can fix that kind of thing. Or even diagnose it. Racing repair is very tough to get into and very expensive and there are few shops to turn to. The sports car repair shop that has a better than average mechanic may tune up a race car for a guy, but it may take three hours to get the carburetors just right, and, at $25 an hour, you may hit the ceiling when you get the bill. But that is part of what racing is all about. You almost have to thank the guy for taking the time to do it right, not be outraged at the $75 bill.

The amount of time a team like Sharp's spends tuning up a car and testing it is impossible to measure in dollars and cents. But you can be sure that they just don't go to a race track on weekends and play with the car. They are there long before the race, practicing and getting everything set up just right. The more professional the team, the more testing time they put in, and it usually pays off because it's worth hours of test time to make sure the half an hour or so you spend on the track during the race is enjoyable. And successful.

There isn't that much track time on weekends, and, when there is, the track is swarming with other cars. If some other guy is in your way every time around the track and you have to keep changing your line, you still won't know whether or not your car is exactly right.

Buying a well-prepared car and taking advantage of the knowledge gained with that particular car can save you a lot of time.

"The biggest mistake most new drivers make at first is that they immediately want more horsepower," says Sharp. "Far more critical to going fast, in turning a fast lap time, and in winning a race and enjoying driving fast is getting the car *handling* right. You'll find guys that will race the same ill-handling pig year after year as they continue buying fancy engine components and saying, 'Oh, if I only had a better camshaft, my car would go faster.' But the answer is to get the car handling so that you can come out of the corner faster and start down the straightaway at a higher rate of speed. It is far more critical than how much the car will accelerate *on* the straightaway. It is exactly how Datsun Zs beat Corvettes: not because they can equal horsepower—they can't—but because they can handle better.

"The average person thinks that the big pedal down there makes all the difference in the world. It doesn't. I mean, why put a five-thousand-dollar engine in a five-thousand-dollar car? A car with regular brakes and shocks and so on. Sure, it will go faster down the straights. But that's it. Period. You're not going to win races, because the guys you're running, who probably won't have as many horses, are going to have better brakes and better suspension, and they're going to beat you."

Mostly Road

If you're going to win in a production class, you need the whole kettle of fish. But even if you just want to get the maximum driving thrill on the highway, you need some changes. Almost every car, for instance, could be improved by adding front and rear sway bars. Not huge bars. There's no reason to completely mess up the comfortable ride, but you want to get rid of a lot of the lean in turns. Even a brand-new 280ZS leans too much in a corner, so it needs sway bars.

If you are going to use the car on the highway, you will probably want to wear out the stock shocks before replacing them—which should take 15,000 miles or so—but install a set of good shocks, such as Konis, just as soon as the car starts floating or porpoising the least bit.

Then put on a set of good tires such as Goodyear Wingfoot, Phoenix 3011s, or Goodrich Radial TA. For a road car, it doesn't make much sense to go beyond those. Sure, you could go the whole route and bolt on Pirelli P7s and go around nearly every corner faster, but it would mean constant work on the highway. The P7s stick so well that you have to drive them every second. Every tar strip will pull the car. For racing, you should use racing tires, which are available at almost every track; but they are not necessary—in fact, they're not even desirable—for highway use.

You definitely need good headlights, such as Cibie or Marchal, and front and rear spoilers might help to a degree, although at highway speeds these are more cosmetic than functional.

"I try to talk most people out of hot-rodding the engine or turbocharging it," says Sharp. "Unless the guy wants a street racer, and unless he's willing to diddle with it once a month. You would be much better off attending to the other things, like wider tires and wheels. Many cars could be improved simply with a little wider tire and wheel, and with a good exhaust system. Headers will help some cars, and you can even keep the catalytic converter with them, but whatever exhaust route you go, do something to relieve some of the back pressure."

A lot can be gained by taking your car to someone who is an expert on that car. Bob Sharp, for example, can drive a person's Datsun Z and immediately tell him six things the car is doing wrong. But he would be hard pressed to tell a person what to do with his Honda or Pontiac. With almost any car, you can find someone who really knows it, so go to the guy who really knows BMWs or Volkswagens if that's what you have. Ask him what you can do to make it a better car; in most cases, the guy owns a car with all the stuff on it, and, if you're lucky, he'll let you drive a car that is right. You may never know the feeling otherwise.

Bill Mitchell begins with tires. "The stock Citation, for example," he says, "has so much rubber in the suspension that without doing a thing to the steering wheel, it could start to change course. It's the leverage factor, and the car sort of takes on an attitude of its own. One of the easiest ways to improve cars like this is through the use of steel-belted radials. You need steel in a front-drive car, merely to minimize slip angle."

Slip angle is the angle the tire assumes before it starts carving out a proper arc. Or, more simply, there are two angles: the angle of the tire as opposed to the angle at which the tire will turn. The difference between the two is the slip angle.

The stiff sidewalls of the steel-belted tire are the ultimate answer to handling. You must take the flex out of the sidewall before you can get any positive results. Knowledge such as this is what keeps Bill Mitchell in business.

"You can't just build a car from a catalog," says Mitchell. "For example, you don't think merely of tires; you must think about tire and wheel combination. Just arbitrarily putting a bigger tire on a car may make it handle worse than before. You may, in some cases, want to go down a size in front for, say, a Camaro, because when you reduce the size of the sidewall, you reduce the flex. It lowers the front end, helping aerodynamically, and it shortens the sidewall. You then can run the car right up against the load limit of the tire and can also run inflation pressures up, which also stiffens the tire and improves the handling without harshening up the ride unduly. And you must make sure that the offset of the rim is proper for your car. Bigger isn't necessarily better. It must be *right* for the car.

"You can go to a fifteen-inch wheel from a thirteen-inch one, getting it up higher; then you go wider with the wheel and maintain the same offset. By using a low-profile tire—say, fifty series—you haven't greatly affected the overall height of the car.

"Maybe smaller is better in some cases," Mitchell points out. "A huge stabilizer bar is usually not necessary. Put on a smaller one in front and try to balance the car with a slightly larger rear bar. It helps to get some rear-wheel steering into the car."

When buying from a catalog, most people invariably will buy *bigger* than stock. Who among us would consider buying something *smaller,* whether it be tires or stabilizer bars, shocks, whatever? The only way some shock manufacturers try to prove their shock is better is by making it super stiff. Heavy duty. They up the stiffness value 20 percent or so and the guy drives away in his buckboard saying, "Yeah, the shocks are good now."

For openers, you have to be pretty clever to do a better job than the factories, so far as the total handling package is concerned. But if you approach the task with some degree of sophistication, keeping in mind what you want the end result to be, you can improve *any* car. You must ask yourself if you want a race car or a racy car. There's a difference. Do you want straightaway speed or faster corner times? Is economy a factor? You must make up your mind, because you can't have it all. That's why they make Ferraris at one end of the scale and diesel Rabbits at the other.

Another important consideration is where you're going to take the car. Who's going to see it? What do you want the car to say about you to others? That can come right back to how shocks are valved or what size stabilizer bars you have.

I have had some cars in my day that my mother refused to ride in—which said something about them—and I've had some that my wife was afraid to drive. You can get carried away. And what *you* might consider really good can be totally impractical. For one thing, it can mean that you're automatically one car short in the family stable.

Again, it boils down to the original question: Are you going to drive a car on the race track or with spirit on the street?

"Starting from the ground up," says Mitchell, "you should probably replace tires, wheels, shocks, stabilizer bars, align the chassis properly, improve lighting, install good lateral support seats, and buy a comfortable steering wheel. Only then should you get into some of the exotics like air dams."

Horns are another important aid, because it's inevitable that if you do all these things to a car, you're going to end up driving it faster, and a horn, like headlights, that can get out farther, can be a real asset. It's defensive. Giving a simple warning to someone who isn't aware of how fast you're going might prevent them from pulling out in front of you.

Most people replace the tires, wheels, shocks, and stabilizer bars and leave out one of the most important parts—the seat. You can put all the suspension improvements in the world into a car, but if you can't stay behind the steering wheel, you can't use them. If you took identical cars and put all the suspension parts in one and only good seats and a good steering wheel in the other, you would probably go faster in the car with the seats and steering wheel, simply because in a tight left-hand turn, the guy with the trick suspension is going to be sitting over in front of the glove compartment. You can't do much of a driving job from over there.

Mitchell encourages his customers to let him install Recaro seats and a good steering wheel; and if the customer insists on keeping the stock items in the car, Mitchell doesn't feel he can properly evaluate the other work he has done. He personally tests every car he builds and says of cars without proper seats and steering, "All I can hope for is that it feels like it has some semblance of handling, and it points in roughly the proper direction."

He can't take the car to the skid pad because all he could do there would be to take right-hand turns, where there's a door to lean against.

"You wouldn't consider racing a car without a good racing seat," he says, "so to drive a car with any spirit on the street without a seat with good lateral support is simply ridiculous."

Mostly Track

Many people decide to go racing by buying a car. To Mitchell this approach is entirely wrong.

"If you really intend to go racing and do a good job at it, buy a bunch of parts," he says. "Don't buy a car. That's the last thing you need. I mean, if you take a look at any competitive road racing car today, very few of the parts that make it go quick in the final analysis are production parts—ones that you would find on the original street-type car.

"All of the people who are really going quick start with a body in white [factory body shell] that has never had any paint or insulation or glue or anything on it. Then they weld in a frame and a roll cage to torsionally stiffen it up. The next thing they do is start on the suspension. They don't use stock bushings and may not even use the stock suspension pickup points —the locations for the control arms—because you can optimize all of that stuff. They would probably change the control arm bushings to bearings, and then add stronger uprights and special brakes."

Mitchell emphasizes that it is very difficult to work progressively from a quick street car to a race car, because most of the people who win are starting from the other direction. They are starting with a pile of parts and building a race car. There is too much insulation on the street car, too many little brackets that you will never use. All of these things add weight, and you will end up with a car that is very heavy. A Camaro, for example, weighs about 3,600 pounds stock, but, built from the ground up as a race car, it might weigh 1,000 pounds less. The heavy one, even with all the performance and handling goodies, might go fast and corner well, but it simply wouldn't be all that competitive against all-out racers.

But keep this in mind: If you're going racing, don't get *too* racy. You can have too much race tire, too much engine, or parts that are too heavy-duty.

To Build or Not to Build

You can't just bolt a 700-horsepower engine into a Corvette, slap on some wide tires, and go racing. It has to be a whole combination. The 700-horsepower motor may get the car down the straightaway in a big hurry, but what happens at the end of the straight? You have to stop, for one thing, and the stock brakes aren't designed to slow the car down from that high speed.

In simple terms, don't make any one element too much more powerful than the others. If you improve the engine's performance by 20 percent, then you had better figure out a way to improve the brakes as well.

There are metallic lining options available that will improve the performance of the brakes; but, like most things, they have their price. The metallic linings squeak like mad and require much more pedal effort. And they usually have to be warmed up before they'll work at all. But, once you do get them working, they work well—much better than the stock linings, which are usually good for one-and-a-half stops from high speed.

You might get by with the relatively new semimetallic linings, which have some of the better characteristics of both metallic and organic linings. They stop much better than stock linings, and they don't squeak as much or require as much pressure as full metallic.

Some of the new GM cars are coming through with semimetallic pads on the inside, callipers and organic on the outside. This is not all that bad a way to go, particularly on a machine you intend to drive on the highway. The manufacturers apparently realize they are in trouble brake-wise or they certainly wouldn't be making a change like that. But it makes sense. The inside pads generally wear out faster because they're in a hotter environment. So with the semimetallic pads, they will not only last longer but will be more resistant to brake fade because they run better hotter. And the organic on the outside gives you a softer pedal and better cold performance. It is one of the few times when you look at a factory change and say to yourself, "Gee, I wish I had thought of that." But then Bill Mitchell did, so perhaps they got the idea from him.

Race Car or Street Car?

The single most important consideration when changing anything on a car is whether you intend to use it for highway or race track. *Establish a plan and make sure the end result will be what you want*—or at least what

BMW magic. There is little resemblance between the street-version BMW and the factory-prepared racer (top and middle), but the extensive modifications—to body and handling—pay off in IMSA action.

you think you are going to use. If you do something to the engine, think about the brakes; if you do something to the handling, don't forget the seats. And think seriously about *this:* If you are going to do things that touch on legality, make sure you are willing to take that risk.

Establish your plan and work toward it progressively. If it is a car that you are going to drive every day, you must enjoy driving it. Just don't get carried away with your changes, like installing a racing clutch instead of a good streetable clutch. Often these items are called "Street and Strip," but stay away from them because in fact they are too much strip and very little street. What you have to compromise on the strip or track means you will probably lose there, too.

Remember, if you are going to spend 90 percent or more of your time on the street, you have a street car, so stay away from anything labelled "strip" or "track." If you are only planning to spend 10 percent or less of your time in competition, anything you put on will work fine.

If you go out to win, however, you are not going to have a street car any more. You are going to be towing it to the track. There is no such thing as a compromise when it comes to winning.

When people decide to buy showroom stock it may be because they drive fast on the highway. One of the first things they do is take the car apart and try to make it go quicker. They charge right into all the racing tricks, like retarding the camshaft, putting in stiffer valve springs, and opening up clearances. These are all things you do to a racing engine to allow it to run at a high rpm, but since you can't put on a bigger carburetor, you waste it all. You wind up with an engine that is set up to run at 7,000 rpm and you are trying to do it all through a little carb. You not only haven't gained anything, you've probably lost something.

Don't build a racing engine unless you are going to put it into a race car. Build the best possible factory engine. Optimize the piston seal; you don't

A Ford Mustang in GT-1 racing trim.

want any blow-by. You don't want any of the little bit of compression you have sneaking down into the pan. You need all you can get up on top. You are only talking about 8:1 because that is all you can legally do in showroom stock class, so you don't have to worry about blown head gaskets or anything like that. What you want to do is minimize piston and cylinder wall clearance, so you don't get into a piston-cocking situation that is going to rob you of horsepower. It is a common error when you start zooping up a showroom stock machine, but if that piston is dragging itself down the cylinder wall, you are losing a lot. Don't go at it as if you were building a race car. It is not a race car, it is a car that is raced. Showroom stock racing is the only class of racing, incidentally, where this is true.

If you get into a real race car, however, you will want to go at it the other way, to loosen things up. But, at the same time, you can have a bigger carburetor and many other things going for you, too. When you cross over that line, that's when you should come from the other direction. Start with a pile of parts, one of which happens to be a body. You build a frame and stick your suspension onto it; then you put on the proper brakes and spindles and the correct hubs and wheels. And when you get through, you don't have a pile of parts to throw away because you didn't have them to begin with. It may seem like a lot more money, but in the long run, it is going to cost you less.

Back in the days when the Group 44 gang with Bob Tullius were running the 12-cylinder Jaguar in D Production class, they were blowing away the Corvettes on a regular basis. There was always a lot of controversy about how their car was illegal and how it shouldn't have been allowed in the class. Well, the way they could have put it all to rest would have been for Group 44 to have built a Corvette the way they built the Jag—from the ground up, from a body in white—taken it out just once and blown the doors off their Jag with it, and then bailed it. They should have shown them what they could do with a real Corvette if they wanted to, because almost every 'Vette raced is merely one that has been bought off a used car lot somewhere, by some guys who immediately start taking things off and bolting new things on.

For that matter, anybody can start with a frame and Chevrolet's performance manual and buy all the stuff they label as "high performance" right over the counter. You don't have to buy a thing you don't need. You can buy a body from one of these guys who makes the whole nose section, and what you end up with is a race car. But it will never be a street machine because it won't have the little things we have all become accustomed to —things like windshield wipers or a heater or turn signals or a top. But it's the way to go racing.

After the major changes are made, you must optimize the minor things. In fact, that is the only point of similarity between street and showroom stock and all the other classes. First, you have to get the wheel bearings to a point where you can spin them and they will just go *shhheeeeooooouuuuu-uuu.* And for racing, keep everything as new as possible. The shocks will wear out a lot faster on the street than they will on a trailer. The same is true of brakes. You want both of them brand new when you get to the track.

Use new oil for each race. If you run on the highway, you subject oil to things like moisture. The short runs, on-and-off improperly warmed-up engine, and so on can cause the oil to sludge, which will result in a slight resistance. And it can load up the plugs. All of these are reasons you see showroom stock cars being towed to a race. Sure they may be pretend race cars, but it still takes this totally different approach if you expect to win.

There are a lot of similarities between showroom stock and a high-performance street car properly and not overly prepared. On both you try to optimize everything from tire pressure to bearing clearance. Shaving tires would be a good practice for either street or showroom stock. Although desperately impractical for the street (you'll be going through tires at a pretty fast rate) it would at least assure you of having perfectly round tires.

The idea is to not only start the race with everything near perfect, but to *finish* the race with everything in that same condition. This means changing wheel bearings for every race, and maybe after practice and qualifying. You should change brake pads at least once during a race weekend. Start out with new pads and change before the race, but make sure the new pads are bedded in. Never start with green linings, or you will finish the race without brakes. You should come up with a schedule. Run the new pads for five laps or so, then pull them out of the car and set them aside for race brakes. Put in another set and do the same thing, using them for practice and qualifying brakes.

You can usually learn more in the pits of a race than you can, for instance, at most local speed shops. Often the guys at the speed shop are not too well informed, and most of them are into the bigger-is-always-better business. Competition clutches are bigger, but there's no way you can push those things in and out for very long and still be able to walk. I mean, can you imagine getting stuck in traffic with one of them? And 12.5:1 compression ratio pistons are fine for a race car, but for the street you can't buy the kind of gasoline they require.

The huge-carburetor syndrome is a similar kind of a bother. Your car has to start all winter long, so you put on this giant carb and it may start at zero, but it isn't going to run very long in weather like that. The gas is going to condense out and form puddles, and it will be first lean and then rich— all over the place.

What usually happens when you put on all this whammy stuff is that you stop *driving* the car. You end up buying some little economy job, and when people ask where your other car is you say, "I only drive it on weekends."

And, the first thing you know, you're not even driving it on weekends. So you wind up with this magnificent machine that might just as well be a mail box.

If it's to be your only car, the reason you are going to put all that money into it is to *enjoy* it. You are not building a car to look at, so it has to be something that will run every day. Every time you get in and turn the ignition key, the car has to start. It's easy to go off the deep end, and there's always someone out there to sell you the wrong stuff, so it takes careful planning to make the right purchases. I happen to have a local Hot Rod shop where the guys know what it takes for a proper street machine, but that's unusual. Make sure *your* shop knows.

If you decide you want the fastest street machine the world has ever seen, that's all well and good—if all you plan to do is drive it once to assure yourself that it's the fastest thing that ever was, and then park it. Think about it.

If, for example, you have your mind set on headers for your Pontiac Firebird, just because your buddy has them on his Camaro, talk to somebody who has them on a Firebird. The exhaust ports on a Pontiac are almost straight down as opposed to the Chevrolet, where they are straight out, so you will end up with pipes so close to the ground that the car will drag on everything. And the pipe will probably hit the frame and you will have to go around explaining what the klunking noise is. The 5 percent performance gain you might pick up could only be worth the bother if you're going to the drag strip. This is but one of many examples of the wrong approach. Always talk with someone who knows.

It takes a lot of discretion to know when to stop. And it takes planning if you're buying a car. What accessories should you have? Well, it used to be when we thought of high performance, we thought of a car without any power-assisted devices at all: no power steering, no power brakes, no power anything. But today you find more and more of the sophisticated cars—even race cars—with power steering. When Tullius raced the big Jag, he had power steering because of the super-wide tires and a power clutch because of the three-plate Borg and Beck clutch in the monster. Why not? The car is so heavy anyway, why not make it easy to drive? This principle definitely holds true for a street machine. Besides, a car with manual steering has a slower steering ratio than one with power, so obviously in a performance-oriented car you want the steering to be as quick as possible. You don't want to have to turn the wheel all over the place just to make a simple maneuver. Most of today's cars that are equipped with power steering still maintain a great deal of their "feel."

Improving Performance

It is extremely difficult to do much and stay legal today. The two go in opposite directions; there's no other way to say it. Now that more and more states are adopting the annual inspection for emissions, you either have to come up with ways to modify a car so that it can be *un*modified once a year or figure out some other way around it.

One of the most significant ways to improve a car's performance is with axle ratio, because most ratios have gone down and down in recent years and today most cars at 60 mph are turning little more than 2,000 rpm, sort of off-idle for a racing engine. So, it only stands to reason, if you want more performance without jeopardizing emissions, one way to get it is by going to a taller axle ratio. It would cost some in terms of economy, but probably not as much as you have been led to believe. It is a little like the *Federales* telling you how much fuel you are going to save by driving 55 mph. It may be true to a point, but it is very hard to prove.

If you drive mostly in town, you will actually get better mileage with a taller axle ratio, where you don't have to step into it so far to get up to 30 or 40 mph. The difference in rpm between two different axle ratios at 35 mph is almost immeasurable. And impossible to detect at the exhaust pipe.

Keep in mind that this and any other changes we list are not necessarily things we suggest you do. You can look on the whole affair as a chronicle of what some *other* people are doing. It merely reflects the philosophy of that NASCAR great, Stroker Ace, who uttered the immortal words, "Cheat neat."

One thing most cars need, as both Bob Sharp and Bill Mitchell note, is a freer flowing exhaust system—duals or headers or whatever, just as long as it offers less back pressure. ANSA, for example, makes a system that is as quiet as stock but reduces the back pressure significantly.

The exhaust is important because it is a starting point for a few other tuning tips. Once you have reduced the back pressure, you can put more timing into it—more spark lead—and you can tune it by ear. Depending on the fuel or octane level you are using, you can adjust the timing level accordingly, trying to optimize that. In many cases, you'll get better economy and better performance, but the exhaust will be dirtier.

"Right around the corner, we're going to have cars with fixed timing," says Mitchell. "So we'll have to get smarter again. In the old days, it was the three C's—cam, carbs, and compression. But today you can't do anything with compression because of the low octane fuel, so that almost rules out anything a cam can do for you. And if you can't do anything with a cam, the carburetion isn't going to do much for you."

You may be getting the picture: The end is in sight if we don't stay a stop ahead of *them*.

One thing you may need to do is rejet the carburetor. Some foreign manufacturers refer to the larger jets as "winterization kits," but whatever one calls them, they will help to remove the hesitation, bucking, and loping of some of the small-engined cars.

You can plug the EGR (exhaust gas recirculation) line effectively, and it will make the engine run a little richer. Since the carburetor is calibrated for a fuel-air mixture including the exhaust gas, it will naturally run richer if you cut off the EGR. And better. Many times one little plug can make quite a difference in performance.

Testing of various jets should be made, trying to make changes just where they are needed. It is useless to richen the mixture through the entire range, just in the slow stuff—the off-idle—leaving the cruising mixture on the lean side. In other words, richen up the power phase, where you stand on it. This effectively does change the mixture all the way through.

"If dual exhaust and axle ratio and desmogging are not satisfactory, then the only answer nowadays is turbocharging," says Mitchell. "Turbocharging can be cleaner, but, unfortunately, not legal unless factory done. As far as the government is concerned, they don't even want you to change an air cleaner element, unless it's made by the manufacturer—an AC element in a GM car. The states, however, are hard-pressed to enforce all of this, so they must resort to the tail-pipe test.

"As far as a turbo is concerned, they can be cleaner than a normally aspirated engine, because you're blowing more air through it. It's even more true on the diesel. And turbocharging is an area where the government has to do some soul-searching. They just rule out everything, and in so doing, they're eliminating a lot of things that could make cars cleaner."

Turbocharging's only drawback, as most people see it, is cost. It is expensive. And it got off to a rather bad start because many of the manufacturers tried to sell it in kit form through magazines and local automotive stores. It requires a very sophisticated installation, and it is not the sort of thing one can do in the driveway.

"The secret of turbocharging is plumbing," Mitchell points out. "Building an exhaust system, rerouting lines, hooking up controls; there's just no way you can get a kit complete enough to include all of these things. I think they're going to have to have installation centers, because it is definitely a job for someone with a good deal of facilities and talent."

Make sure that you know what you are doing or that the guy who is doing it for you has the experience and the tools, because there is nothing worse than a poorly turbocharged car. It could become totally undrivable.

3

Specific Modifications

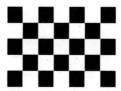

We have taken a look at the basics of building a race car as compared to improving the performance of a highway machine or a showroom stock racer, and we have looked at some ways to improve engine performance. Along the way, we have talked about a few things that can be done to improve the handling of almost any car—shocks, tires and wheels, sway bars, lighting, exhaust, seats, and steering wheel—and I wouldn't suggest that the average car enthusiast do anything else to a highway or a showroom stock car. Or even some production classes unless you are very serious.

So let's take a look at some specifics about these modifications, with information from the people who make what many consider to be the best products in the world—Koni shocks, Phoenix tires, Enkei wheels, Marchal and Cibie lighting, Hooker headers, ANSA exhaust systems, Recaro seats, and Momo and Lecarra steering wheels. As for sway bars, it is pretty much an individual situation, determined by the type of car.

Shock Absorbers

Jan Zuijdijk, chief engineer for Koni America and an expert on shock absorbers, quickly points out that the name of the object itself is a mistake, and so are a lot of other ideas about this critical part of your suspension.

Specific Modifications

"They do *not* absorb shocks," says Zuijdijk. "What they do is actually convert kinetic energy, produced by motion, into thermal energy, or heat. In most shock absorbers, this is accomplished by moving a piston connected to the body of the car through a cylinder filled with oil or some other fluid. The cylinder, fluid, and its reservoir are connected to the axle or suspension of the car and move with the wheel it serves. The action of shock absorbers is to diminish—or to dampen—this motion. So shock absorbers should, more properly, be called dampers. Which they are in Europe."

These dampers control two kinds of movements. First is the oscillation of the car's unsprung weight—the wheels, control arms, etc.—caused by the tires rolling over the surface of the road, which is never perfectly flat. Also, rolling tires act as air springs with a high natural frequency.

The second kind of motion controlled by the shock absorbers occurs when the wheels roll over a bump in the road and the springs are compressed against the mass of the car. Compressed, the springs react by trying to restore the ride height of the car. If this restorative movement went uncontrolled by shock absorbers, the energy stored in the compressed springs would push the body of the car past its normal static position—the ride height. Then the car would sag back below ride height. This up-and-down motion, undampened, would repeat over and over again, with the risk that the tires would fail to maintain contact with the road and the driver would lose control of his vehicle.

The main function of a shock absorber, therefore, is to stop this motion and thus to maintain the tire/road contact at all times. This is done by what is called "rebound damping force," created when the shock absorber is being pulled in extension.

A few brands of shock absorbers, Koni among them, are infinitely adjustable, which makes it possible for engineers to select the precise adjustment to achieve the right balance between comfort and handling in a car. This adjustability is possible through a combination of the number and diameter of bores, an adjusting nut at the end of the piston rod that can alter the spring load on the valve and also close off a few piston rod orifices, and the kind of valve employed.

There are two features that every shock absorber should have, regardless of type or manufacturer. First is longevity, a constant level of performance over a long life span. Second is the right "characteristic" for the suspension of which it is part.

It is the characteristic of a shock absorber which most manifests itself to the driver and passengers of a car. Each car, having a suspension system that has been designed for it, requires shock absorbers with a characteristic which is proper for that suspension system.

Over their lifetime, most original equipment dampers gradually lose their effective damping ability, requiring replacement, or adjustment if they are of the high quality of manufacture that permits adjustment. It is difficult to give a set of guidelines on how to determine when a shock absorber has lost its effective damping because many cars are underdampened in manufacture, and since the "wear" is gradual, the loss of damping performance is not perceptible. However, a few simple observations can help make a determination about the condition of shock absorbers.

First, check the condition of the shock visually. Look for oil leakage, broken or worn mounting parts, and bent or rusted piston rods.

Second, consider the mileage since the last replacement or since the car was bought. Most original equipment and inexpensive dampers are completely worn out after just 15 to 20,000 miles; and long before that mark, the damping performance has become marginal at best.

It is the behavior of your car that is the best indicator of your shocks' condition. A sure sign of deterioration is if the chassis touches the rubber bump stops frequently with only a moderate load in the car. Excessive body roll or lean when cornering, difficulties in keeping the car in a straight line when a side wind is prevalent, steering wheel vibrations and wheel-hop on rough surfaces, all indicate a problem with the shock absorbers.

Shock absorbers are strongly safety-related. If they are worn and the car owner does not recognize the signs, he may suddenly find himself in serious trouble when an emergency occurs. Worn dampers reduce tire-road contact drastically, resulting in longer braking time, easy skidding under braking, and minimal control just when it is needed most.

All Koni shocks can be adjusted to re-set the damping forces after use to like-new performance, or to satisfy the car enthusiast who prefers handling to comfort. For race and rally purposes, Koni, as well as others, has developed dampers that can be adjusted externally, without being removed from the car.

Shock absorbers can be used to influence such aspects of handling as understeer, oversteer, pitch, etc.—qualities that are critical on and off the circuit. The purpose of a shock absorber on a race car is to provide just as much damping as is necessary for easy control, but no more.

Too much damping in compression will cause the wheels and tires to jump over bumps in the road, reducing traction because of wheel spin.

Too much rebound force at the rear suspension will cause oversteer. Too much rebound force at the front will cause the opposite, understeer. This is the case especially when the basic setting allows a fair amount of damping in the lower piston velocity range—low-speed damping—because it affects the roll rate in the same way an anti-roll bar does.

In shock absorbers, as in everything else in life, you get what you pay for. If you want to get shock absorbers of quality and longevity, there is one rule to follow: Select the manufacturer who will use the best materials available, keep tolerances as small as possible, and employ rigid quality control of parts and the finished product.

Specific Modifications

Lighting

John Champion, sales coordinator for SEV Corporation, the American outlet for Cibie (pronounced *C-B-A*) and Marchal lights says that beam pattern, optical accuracy, and quartz-halogen bulbs are the three most important aspects of lighting for any performance machine.

"The beam pattern," Champion says, "is the shape of the light as it's projected from your lamp. And, since different beam patterns allow you to see different things, the beam pattern is the most important characteristic to consider when selecting your lamps.

"The lens is responsible for spreading the light into a computer-calculated beam pattern developed for specific driving conditions. An intricate prism configuration on the inside of the lens bends the light to the needed degree as it passes through the glass. This is called beam control.

"Since truly effective nonglaring illumination can only result from precision beam control, we put a lot of emphasis on the production of our lenses. They're all made from the finest lead crystal glass, having optimum light transmission properties, and they're checked with a laser beam for optical accuracy. This is a very costly process, but with a component as important as our lens, we just can't afford to compromise. Don't forget, with ineffective lighting, you'll pay the really high cost of poor visibility."

A quartz-halogen lamp produces its characteristic bright, white light because the filament burns at a much higher temperature than a conventional bulb or sealed beam lamp. Conventional bulbs cannot operate at these temperatures because the glass is not designed to withstand such high heat levels and will shatter. In addition, conventional bulbs, after turning awhile, will deposit particles on the inside surface of the bulb, causing it to discolor. This reduces the effective range and produces dimmer, more yellow, and less efficient road lighting.

But good lighting performance requires more than a bright bulb. That's important, of course, but it's only the beginning. All the light in the world is no good if it's not directed where you need it, when you need it. Consider trying to drive by the light of a movie projector. Despite its fantastic output, its beam pattern is totally useless as a driving lamp.

What about candlepower ratings? Since they are only a measure of basic light output, and not beam effectiveness, they really don't tell you very much. In addition, there are several commonly accepted ways to measure candlepower, with each one providing different, often widely varying readings. So unqualified candlepower figures are actually meaningless and can be deceptive and misleading.

Above is an actual photo of conventional 7" sealed beam headlights in use. Restricted forward range makes the pedestrian hard to see. Poorly distributed light results in "hot spots" that make driving uncomfortable and tiring. The bottom photo illustrates the greatly extended range available with "Z Beam" headlights as well as their broad, even illumination for reduced eyestrain and a better view of the shoulder areas. The pedestrian at 200 feet is boldly visible. (Photos courtesy Cibie.)

For really effective, usable illumination, all the components of the lamp must work together like a team. The slightest imperfection in the lens or reflector can block or scatter the light from even the best bulb, causing greatly reduced visibility and increased glare. In that case, the lamps just won't do the job you bought them to do.

Lighting for night racing or rallying is even more critical, points out Mitch Williams, coordinator of performance activities for SEV.

"The job a headlight has to do at night is difficult and it will never be perfect," says Williams, "but it had better be very good because a racer is always on the edge of out-driving his lights. Those corners come very quickly at night and you need all the help you can get."

This is precisely why lights such as Cibie and Marchal are so important to high-speed driving. They are precision optical instruments, engineered and tested by the most sophisticated laboratory techniques, and proven at the world's toughest competitive events. The result? Unparalled optical accuracy. And that's the true measure of lighting performance. Unfortunately, in their divine wisdom, some states still do not allow them because they are not sealed beam units. The inspectors don't look at the important aspects of the lighting; nor do they consider the fact that if the lens shatters, the lamp will still work, creating a tremendous safety factor. So, check local regulations or save your old handy-dandy American sealed beam units. They may come in handy at inspection time.

Exhaust Systems

All performance experts agree that an exhaust system that relieves some of the back pressure is an advantage, both to power and economy. There are many fine systems on the market. ANSA, for example, makes a complete line of systems that bolt right on, muffler and all, in a matter of minutes. And, importantly, they don't make the car sound like a "hot rod" of the '60s. You can keep the catalytic converter, which makes the Feds deliriously happy, and it won't hamper the performance all that much.

Or you can go the whole route and bolt on a set of headers. But, as I said before, first talk with someone who has them on a car exactly like yours. They can be extremely bothersome if they alter the ground clearance of the car or if they slam and bam every time you hit a bump. And make sure you buy headers that are made by a recognized firm.

Hooker Industries makes headers for almost every American and imported car. Its president, Dave Spangler, had this to say: "It is generally well accepted by most people who really know about cars that the installation of a well-designed set of headers is the best place to start improving the performance of any vehicle. It is also accepted that when increases in horsepower are achieved, improvement in fuel economy is usually a by-product.

"Well-engineered headers are designed to create an optimum pressure balance between the intake and exhaust systems. Properly designed headers actually use the exhaust waves to expel all the burnt gases from the combustion chamber and draw in the maximum fresh charge of fuel and air. The result is a more potent combustion cycle producing horsepower gains and better mileage.

"Unfortunately, accurate specifications for a *tuned* exhaust system are not determined by some mysterious mathematical formula or by a sophisticated computer. There are formulas, and computers can be of assistance, but in the final analysis a good deal of *cut and try and test again* still goes into a *tuned* exhaust system."

The objective of an optimum exhaust system is to cause a complete cleaning or blow down of the chamber during the exhaust stroke, allowing maximum capacity for the fresh charge of fuel and air to be introduced during the intake stroke. In engines with long duration of *valve overlap* (the period during which both intake and exhaust valves are opened simultaneously), it is possible to overscavenge the combustion chamber, inadvertently exhausting some of the unburned fresh charge.

However, in tuning the exhaust system for a particular application, many additional factors must be taken into consideration. Factors such as vehicle weight, gear ratio, and probable end-use are among many other variables that play an important part in determining the ideal rpm at which peak torque should be developed. Primary pipe diameter is the most influential factor here, while primary pipe length can be used to move the curve around this peak, taking torque from one rpm and putting it in another.

"As is readily apparent by now," adds Spangler, "header development is a complicated and expensive affair. Not all manufacturers are willing to take the time or spend the money. While most headers available today will provide improvement over stock cast-iron manifolds, there are significant differences."

In addition to fuel-saving, headers will cause the engine to be more sensitive to subsequent modifications such as improvement in the intake manifold, carburetor, and ignition systems.

Although each case will be different, some improvement in performance and fuel consumption will usually result from the installation of headers. It is not uncommon to experience fuel economy improvements within the range of 10–20 percent and in some cases even higher. Performance improvement expressed in quarter-mile acceleration time and speed are usually two-tenths to a full second quicker, with top speed at the end of the quarter-mile often increasing by 2 to 5 miles per hour. More subjectively, the headers will probably be responsible for a better "feel" to the vehicle, better response, and more direct acceleration.

"The headers will work alone," Spangler notes. "But, for many people who don't intend to stop there, they will allow the full cumulative benefit to be realized from later modifications. Improvements in fuel economy in excess of a hundred percent have been found with combinations of external engine modifications."

For maximum effect, a relatively large-diameter dual exhaust system with low restriction mufflers is preferred, in conjunction with the headers. The crossover pipe will sometimes improve low rpm torque and help control excessive noise.

However, as most of you are aware, many later-model vehicles are equipped with single exhaust systems and catalytic converters. Experience indicates that the catalytic converter is not significantly restrictive. Although expensive, it might be best to convert to a dual exhaust system utilizing two converters. But thorough and well-documented testing has shown that headers remain beneficial to engine performance even when used with a catalytic converter and single exhaust system. Furthermore, it is conceivable that with this combination the converter is required to do less work for reasons of increased efficiency imparted by the headers.

The performance and fuel economy test results presented below are for a 1975 Chevy Nova equipped with Hooker headers in conjunction with the original single exhaust system and converter. The vehicle had a 350-cubic-inch engine and automatic transmission.

	Stock	With Headers	
Gas mileage (mpg)	12.76	14.72	(+15.3%)
¼-mile acceleration			
E.T. (seconds)	16.81	16.31	(−.50)
M.P.H.	82.30	84.77	(+2.47)

Emission tests were also conducted. They showed improvement in CO and NO_x emissions, and although HC emissions were increased, they remained well below the applicable California and federal standards. It is possible to produce better performance, improve fuel mileage, and still take part in cleaning up the environment.

The test numbers for the 1975 Nova presented above resulted from the simple bolt-on application of headers. However, as was stated earlier, the headers will cause the engine to be more sensitive to other modifications. Often the combination of headers with the appropriate high-performance manifold, carburetor, and ignition system, along with a good tune-up, will produce incredible results. At the minimum, carburetor jetting should be checked to verify the proper fuel/air mixture.

"I have heard several people expound on the many virtues of a finely tuned exhaust system for race cars and in the same breath suggest that shortcuts can be taken in the development of headers for the street," says Spangler. "Their contention is that, among other things, the low-compression ratios and restrictive exhaust systems of most street engines render them less sensitive to a proper header design. On the contrary, the benefits to be realized from the fine tuning of sound pressure waves in a mildly tuned or less powerful street engine are even more important. The variables are more numerous and the time and expense required much greater. However, the benefits to be derived from a proper street exhaust system are substantial."

Seating and Steering Wheel

A really good automobile seat with a lot of lateral support not only keeps you in the proper place, but it gives the needed back support on long trips. And, if properly designed, it is safer in a crash because it won't break away from the anchorage points.

As with headers and almost every other performance-related product, there are several good seats made throughout the world. Unfortunately, few production automobiles offer them as standard equipment. Porsche is an exception; they install Recaro seats in all of their cars.

David Schwartz of the American branch of the German-based Recaro company said, "All of our seats are anatomically shaped, formulated through extensive medical research by orthopedic surgeons. The result is optimum support at the upper back, lower hips, legs, and sides of the torso.

"They provide lateral support, which eliminates fatigue and strain due to unnecessary muscular tension. Simply put, you don't have to fight to stay in your seat when cornering."

Many agree with Schwartz. The editors of *Car and Driver* magazine recently conducted extensive road tests to compare six of the leading after-market seats with stock Pontiac Firebird bucket seats. In each case, they found the replacement seats better than the original equipment.

Following the road tests on California's Ortega Highway, the magazine

Seats such as this Recaro can add greatly to your ability to control a car.

reported: "The Recaro Model N in this test missed a perfect across-the-board score by a single point in just one category. One tester considered thigh support a bit lacking, but otherwise this seat thrilled us both like no other.

"It's so good that all the other seats—the Scheel included [which they rated second, incidentally]—aren't even close. The Recaro happened to be the last seat in our test sequence, and after hammering up and down Ortega Highway for one long, hard-driving day, these buckets felt like balm for our backsides.

"The Recaro's foam-padded upholstery meets your bottom with the firm assurance that it's not about to let you shuffle around where you shouldn't. . . . Instead of wallowing in lumps of squishy foam, you sit squarely on a solid base that feels perfectly matched to the back contours of your torso. The side bolsters don't pressure you in straight-line driving, but as you lean into lateral restraint in the turns, the side wings grasp you securely, like a catcher's mitt around a baseball."

Interesting, to say the least, since they are comparing an after-market seat with one of the better original equipment seats available. It helps to prove that we need something more than is offered by most original equipment seats. And if you can't plunk down the $800 or so that a basic pair of Recaros cost, there are other good seats to be had for less. If you do have the shekels, though, spend them on a really good seat. You can transfer it from car to car as you trade, simply by purchasing a new mounting kit. Just remember to keep the original seats so you can put them back in the old buggy when you trade it in.

As for steering wheels, some cars have good ones. Most don't. A steering wheel should have spokes at the 3 o'clock and 9 o'clock positions, so that you can position your hands properly when cornering at high speeds. There should be no restrictions to prevent you from locking-in your thumbs around the spokes. Beyond that, the rim of the wheel should be large enough in diameter so that you can get a good grip on it. And it should be padded for better control and comfort. Leather is best. Look at any good race car or really outstanding road machine, and you will find exactly this type of wheel.

Ferrari, for example, uses Momo steering wheels on all of their cars, and, being a Ferrari nut, I consider the Momo to be the best. But, in testing, I found that there are many other good ones. Lecarra, to our delight, makes not only a fine wheel but an aesthetically pleasing one. And they make it for everything from a Volkswagen to a Peterbuilt. The model we tested on our diesel Rabbit was gold anodized with brown leather, a stunning combination. So the steering wheel doesn't necessarily have to have the stark appearance of an Indianapolis race car model. It, like good seats, can actually add to the appearance of your car.

Wheels and Tires

The basic reason that most people immediately change wheels and tires on a performance machine is that those mounted on almost every production car are designed to give maximum service at the lowest possible cost to the manufacturer. In most cases, they are bought from the lowest bidder. You certainly don't want that thought racing through your mind as you careen around a windy mountain highway.

It makes no particular difference which you buy first, tires or wheels, but either way, they should be matched to each other. And definitely talk with someone who can tell you what to select for the type of driving you intend to do.

The size of the after-market wheel (or rim as the manufacturers prefer to call it) is determined, obviously, by the size of the tire. A wider tire will require a wider rim. What could be more basic advice than that? But, just as vital, are the following questions: How important is the cosmetic value? How maintenance-free do you want them to be? How will they affect the car's suspension? Will they improve performance?

A lighter wheel *will* help in performance because most stock wheels contribute significantly to the car's unsprung weight. Lightening the weight connected to the springs can help keep the car's suspension working properly. We tested a set of aluminum Enkei modular-type wheels, distributed by Golden Wheel, and found them to work fantastically well, in addition to adding the proper cosmetic touch.

Modular wheels are standard to racing because they are light *and* strong. They feature an inner and outer rim, bolted to a hub, and allow the versatility of changing rim width without buying a complete new wheel. It is an expensive but highly satisfactory way to go. In the case of the Enkei and many other modular-*type* wheels, the construction is the same but the pieces are welded and/or riveted together.

There are dozens of fine wheels on the market, so it is a relatively easy task to match a set to your requirements of size, looks, weight, upkeep, and strength. Just don't get carried away with *width.* The offset of the wheel is tremendously important because it can completely change the handling characteristics of your car. That ultra-wide-track look can move the wheel's center-line so far outboard that the result could be dangerous in a turn. If you can't get satisfactory answers from your local tire or wheel supplier, don't be afraid to call the manufacturers. They should have an expert, and it is certainly worth the price of a long distance phone call.

In our case, we got solid information from Joel Miller of Meon, Inc., the American distributor for Phoenix tires, and from Chuck Dressing of Tire America.

"A wheel like the Enkei," said Dressing, "gives you strength and durability as well as lightness, and the aluminum dissipates the heat quickly, improving brake performance. Wheels and wheel covers absorb a tremendous amount of heat under normal operating conditions. At high speeds, this excess heat may cause brake failure by brake fade, so it makes aluminum highly desirable in a wheel."

Of all the tires tested, the Phoenix Stahlflex 3011 (made in Germany) was the best in adhesion, and can be highly recommended for street, solo, and showroom stock. But, close behind was Goodyear's Wingfoot. Then came the Goodrich T/A Radial.

The biggest question then becomes: Road tire or race tire? And the answer is exactly the same as with car preparation. If you are going racing, use racing tires. If it is to be a road machine, use road tires. In showroom stock you can get by with a really good road tire like the Phoenix, but there still is nothing like a racing tire for racing.

There is such a vast difference in controllability in turns, and if you find yourself mixing it up with race-tire-equipped cars on a tight road course, you are going to come out on the short end. For one thing, race tires are lighter and dissipate heat more rapidly. And, since heat build-up is the biggest single enemy of any tire, you have automatically eliminated a major cause of tire failure. Sure, you can shave off some of the tread rubber and accomplish roughly the same thing, but who wants to grind away all that expensive rubber? Besides, a racing tire has a thinner sidewall as well, and that, too, helps to get rid of a lot of the heat. Just don't go the other way, because racing tires simply won't work on the street. The thin sidewalls are dangerous anywhere you might encounter curbs or rocks or whatever.

A new driver probably should start with a slightly harder tread compound in a racing tire. There really isn't much of a choice as to brand, since Goodyear is about the only American manufacturer left building racing tires for most types of cars. Besides, Goodyear wrote the book on many phases of racing tire development, and they have experts at nearly every race to advise you on the proper tire for your car.

"It's important to start with a conservative racing tire," says Reed Kryder of Goodyear. "We make all types of compounds [the particular batch of tread rubber], from relatively hard to super-sticky. But, when starting, the first thing you want to do is just get in the laps, to get the feel of things. You need so many hours of track time, so what you should be after these first days is reliability and longevity. A harder compound will give you that."

It makes sense, because the tire bill can be terrifying to the beginner. With a lighter production car you might get as many as eight weekends out of a set of tires, but as you move up to the faster and heavier classes, it goes down to one or two. And when you really get fast, it becomes one or two sets a weekend. So you want to get as much experience as possible out of that first set or two of tires.

For street or solo or rally, there is no question, the Pirelli P7 is the standard. But these are *so* sticky that you have to drive the car every inch of the way. There is no time to relax. And the $300 or $400 a tire price tag might eliminate a lot of prospective buyers.

According to a recent *Car and Driver* test, the Phoenix "is far and away the best dry tuner of the bunch. It was a joy to drive on the skidpad where it not only beat the P7 but also made the Mustang feel delightfully neutral . . . we still recommend this tire to all street, slalom, and Showroom Stock racers in the crowd because it can turn ordinary cars into g-machines."

There obviously are many other good tires, such as the Goodrich Radial T/A and the Goodyear Wingfoot, but make sure that whatever tire you buy is a performance tire. Make sure it has been developed, and thoroughly tested, for high speed and for wet and dry cornering. The tire is either the first or the final link with the pavement, depending upon where you start.

Project Car

After listening to the advice of some of the world's foremost automotive performance experts, it was inevitable that I would want to put some of the ideas to work, so I decided to build a project car, a *practical* road machine. And, having owned a few Hondas over the years, I decided to start with an Accord LX, a car with which I was highly familiar in stock configuration.

To many, it might sound absolutely ludicrous to imagine a Honda as a scaled-down BMW or to think of making it into a Lotus-like road machine. But we set out to prove the point.

When the new Accord arrived, it was like greeting an old friend. Until I got to the first traffic light. When the light turned green, I nailed it, and it coughed, did a sort of hula, coughed again. And died. Could I have forgotten how to drive a Honda? Not a chance. After all, it was my fourth one. Next time the light turned green, I let out the clutch with a little less alacrity, trying not to look stupid twice in one block. It lurched again. "Hesitation," I said to myself, realizing that my work was cut out for me.

Back at the Honda dealership, I was told, "You're standing at the end of a long, long line, pal. Try unleaded gas, it'll take away the . . . uh, the . . ."

"Hesitation," I said.

"Yeah, hesitation. It'll take some of it out."

Unleaded gas, indeed. One of the reasons I drove Accords was so that I could run *regular* gas. So I lurched my way home, consoling myself along the way with the knowledge that the '78 hadn't been as smooth as the '77, which, in turn, seemed slightly less silky than the '76. Also, that many current cars suffer the same problems, and I had gotten used to each of them.

After a couple hundred miles of hesitation, I turned to the classified section, which I always do after all else has failed. It comes right after reading the instructions. If nothing else, the classifieds convince me that I'm not the only one out there who is a shade less talented than George Bignotti. And, sure enough, there it was under Section 250. Parts. "A/T Engineering. Unturbocharge Your Honda." What the ad said was that for less money than a turbocharger I could have more power than with a blower and wouldn't melt pistons or any of those mundane things. But what about hesitation?

A call to Serge Harabosky at A/T eased my mind. The Stage One modification was what I needed. It would, I was told, smooth it out, add a few horses, and make it more fun.

A few days later I was on my way to New Milford, Connecticut, skeptical but hopeful. Somehow it seemed too simple.

After a couple of Wattneys at Harabosky's neat little hop-up-your-Honda store, we tackled the problem. Apparently the Honda folk, in an admirable attempt to build the cleanest-burning engine in the world, had moved directly to 1985 EPA standards. It is the sort of thing that makes people in Washington gleeful, but it is also the kind of move that leans out an engine to the point that not even Richard Petty could shift it smoothly.

We replaced the stock cam with a dual pattern A/T cam, designed to greatly improve the acceleration and hill-climbing ability of the car. With a .375 lift and a .282 duration. Which should increase performance. You've probably already figured out that you're not getting a full-blown technical project report. Instead you're getting an absolutely *non*technical, no-frills driver impression of a simple solution to a motoring problem that is not restricted to Hondas.

We took off the stock coil and plug wires and added Accel Super Coil and Accel ignition wires, and then we rejetted the carburetor. This latter task was supposed to have been done by the dealer, but somehow it was overlooked. So we took a Honda jetting kit (reference number H/C 79216) and installed it, richening it up a bit by giving the main jet three twists out.

Replacing the cam and rejetting the carb had given us more torque. The Accel coil and wires had increased the spark. The larger jets gave us the fuel/air mixture we needed. To keep the handling characteristics in line with the increase in performance, we added a three-quarter-inch rear sway bar and replaced the stock front three-quarter-inch sway bar with a one-inch bar. It all took three hours.

Project Honda: The Accord LX (above) turned out to be a sort of mini BMW with the Phoenix tires, Enkei wheels, trick suspension, Koni shocks, Cibie and Marchal headlights, ANSA exhaust, A/T Engineering cam, and other goodies. Note (below) the Recaro seats, Momo steering wheel, and, finally, the Fuzzbuster (radar detector) just to make sure it doesn't all land you in front of the local magistrate.

Most front drive cars are inherently understeering to begin with. They tend to have a lot of body roll, so you have to try to minimize these understeer characteristics, which definitely means a rear bar. And a larger bar in front is a step in the right direction. It might be wise to stick with the standard front bar and add a rear bar and try it. Then, if that's not enough, enlarge the front one.

It is often tough to do these things step-by-step, but it is an interesting exercise to see the difference. In the case of the Honda, it needed a larger front bar.

Specific Modifications

Step-by-step is wise in any modification. Often we go straight from mild to wild and wind up with a car that performs beautifully, but it is a car you can't drive on the streets any more. You get in the car and find you can't even make it out of your driveway because it has no power at all in the everyday driving range. You don't really want this, particularly in a little car that has very little low-end torque simply because of the small displacement.

We could have bolted on new heads and manifold and big Webers, but that would have required revving the engine to four grand and then slipping the clutch all the way up to three just to get away from the stop sign. So, for once we used our heads and opted for the milder modification.

Then we went out to road test the car. On some pretty windy Connecticut back roads.

I eased the car down to the main highway—Connecticut Route 67 toward Roxbury. I was ecstatic after a couple of smooth take-offs from traffic lights in New Milford, and I was astounded when I got out of town and really nailed it. The performance was unbelievable, and the hesitation was gone. When we got to the first section of tight road, I became a true believer. The new sway bars had leveled out the handling to the point where it felt for a minute like I was driving a Porsche. Well, maybe an RX-7. In a couple of millenniums of bolting things onto cars, these sway bars were the first things that had ever worked better than promised. And for only a tad over $300.

The superior handling only whetted my appetite. I went to the Koni shock absorber plant in Culpepper, Virginia, and had a set of Konis fitted. I was suddenly at Stage II, because the Konis flattened it out even more in the corners. Everything you've always heard about them is true.

The most surprising aspect of the whole episode was the gas mileage on my Accord following the conversion. On the trip back to West Virginia I averaged a whopping 33.22 miles per gallon. At Fuzzbuster-protected speeds. Extensive testing of combined highway/city driving produced 27.45 miles per gallon. Both of these figures were nearly 2 miles per gallon *higher* than anything I had ever gotten with the stock machine.

Now I was hooked on the project. I had improved the handling, smoothed out the acceleration, and increased the overall performance. And improved the gas mileage. On regular gas, if you please. Naturally I didn't stop there. I contacted ANSA and got my hands on one of their neat-looking, twin chrome outlet exhaust systems. "The exhaust Ferrari fits," it said on the UPS package. It took twenty minutes to install.

Again performance went up, and the gas mileage jumped to 34.76 highway and 28.24 combined. Moreover, the ANSA system proved to be as quiet as the stock system, with just some occasional popping to remind us that we weren't driving around in a strictly stock machine. It may be all we have left.

Next I looked at oil additives. Tephguard, according to the ad, is the lubricant of the '80s, an oil additive with Teflon. It also claimed it would increase my gas mileage. Why not? I added it to the Valvoline oil. And increase the mileage it did, from 34 to 36.80 highway and 31.42 combined.

Even with the suspension changes, there was still something missing. It took me several days of four-wheel drifting through the back roads around my farm to decide that the stock Michelin XZX tires weren't keeping up with the under-carriage improvements. We mounted a set of Goodyear Wingfoot radials, stepping up from 165-R13s to 185s. It was a definite improvement, but still not what we wanted, so I called the Phoenix people.

A set of Phoenix Stahlflex 3011s in 205/60R 13 mounted on Super-neat Enkei 6-inch wheels, absolutely glued the car to the highway. In fact, I was so damned excited about the handling characteristics of the car that I decided to go the whole route and bolt in a set of Recaro seats and a Momo steering wheel.

And it was just as Bill Mitchell had said. The seats and the steering wheel were as important to handling as some suspension parts. So I further took his advice on lighting and horns and installed Cibie headlights and Marchal air horns.

What I had now was an incredibly responsive and practical road machine.

I had become totally engulfed by the project, so I called a friend in Miami, Charlie Brown, a retired Air Force colonel who has developed what he calls an engine air-conditioner. His Power Pak is a simple but, as I was to learn, an effective device, consisting of a ceramic cone with a venturi in the center, through which air is channeled to the carburetor. The cone is incapsulated in a plastic sleeve filled with water (with a reservoir to keep it filled). The porous ceramic provides air to the carburetor of such density that it is like driving on a rainy day. Every day. In fact, the Power Pak is said to "humidify at 90 percent plus factor at highway speeds, which will achieve the highest gain in gas mileage and power."

And humidify it did. It humidified that rascal right past the magical 40-mile-per-gallon mark. To 41.65 highway, 34.20 combined. And dynamometer tests indicated we had *lowered* emissions. Washington take note.

Now the interesting part: The Accord accelerates from zero to 60 in 10.45 seconds, which is nearly 3 full seconds quicker than stock. And all of this will work on almost any car.

Cosmetically, we added a trick paint scheme, a rear spoiler, replaced the stock hood with a four-door Honda hood, which eliminated the hood ornament and smoothed out the front edge contour, and we fitted an Auto-plas rear window louver. With the wider stance and squatter appearance, the Accord looks surprisingly like a Lotus relative.

The entire exercise produced a sports sedan for just under $10,000, which may seem a little steep for a Honda, but two minutes behind the wheel will cause even the most skeptical to agree that the basically mild-mannered sedan has been transformed into a mini BMW. And the same thing can be done to any number of cars—American, German, and Japanese alike. Almost any of the changes alone will delight you; and all of them together will astound you.

4

High-Performance Driving—
Road and Track

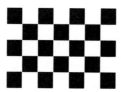

Perhaps this chapter should begin with the immortal words of race driver Stroker Ace: "If you're ever going to stand on it at all, stand on it now. The longer you wait, the slower you get."

That says it all.

But, before you "stand on it," you must know the one thing required of all race drivers—car control. If you are going to drive a race car, you will need car control 100 percent of the time; if you intend to drive well and safely on the highway, you may need it only 30 or 40 seconds a year, but you will need it very badly during this brief period.

Think of it as *maximum* car control, this ability to drive a car at the limit; but don't, whatever you do, limit it strictly to high speeds. A lot of this skill can be applied to everyday driving conditions, *below* the speed limit, to make you a safer and better driver. And it certainly can add a lot more zest to your driving experience.

With this in mind, let us examine in detail some techniques that, although generally prescribed for the race course, will work nicely on the highway as well. Almost all of them will put more fun into your driving, particularly on that section of twisting, turning back road you have always wanted to

A Turbo Porsche in Daytona 24-hour competition trim.

master. And if you intend to race, it will move you a giant step closer to the winner's circle.

Three words essentially describe the art of driving a car quickly and safely: *smoothness, consistency,* and *concentration.*

Smoothness: Everything you do in a car, from how you operate the controls to your overall attitude, should be as smooth as you can possibly make it. This is essential. But you will find that smoothness becomes increasingly more difficult as your speed goes up, so it is important to start at low speed and get everything working perfectly before moving on. Become smooth at 30 or 40 miles per hour and increase the speed in small increments, continuing that smoothness as you go faster and faster.

Simply use the word as an adjective for everything you are doing; smoothly squeeze on the brakes, feed in the steering smoothly, shift smoothly. Don't be rough with the car and throw it around; what you are trying to do is balance the car on all four tire patches as evenly as possible, all the time. It requires finesse.

Consistency: Always do things the same way, whether executing a very simple maneuver like sitting in the car or using the brake and throttle in a proper downshift. Become a machine yourself. And don't get discouraged if you find yourself consistently doing the same thing *wrong.* At least, it means you have the ability to do the same thing more than once. You can always go back to Square One, correct the technique, and become consistent in the proper technique.

The worst thing you can do is take a corner or make a shift or brake differently each time. Consistency is the one aspect of high-performance driving that can be measured. In lap times. A good race driver can lap a track, not varying more than half a second per lap for 50 or 100 laps—or whatever it takes. To do that he must do everything exactly the same way, every lap. The dangerous driver is the one who goes out and breaks the track record on one lap and is then 2 seconds slower on the next one. For one thing, it was probably sheer luck that allowed him to break the record in the first place, and he may not even come around for a third lap. He can't know exactly where he is braking or turning; and with different inputs, there are always different results. Some of them can be disastrous. You don't exit a corner at 130 miles per hour with some sort of vague idea of how you did it before.

Concentration: It takes 100 percent mental discipline to drive a car really well. Mistakes can be covered up at slow speeds, but not at high speeds. Racing is not a forgiving sport. You may not be around to go back and analyze a spin as you would a bad punt, so it is imperative that you concentrate fully the first time. And every time. Eliminate everything else from your mind, relax, and concentrate fully on your driving.

Mastering the Car

A great deal of what you are about to read will seem elementary, but when you put it all together you will find that you and your car have a much better rapport with each other. You will know what the car is doing underneath you, and that is the first step toward becoming an outstanding driver —on or off the track.

The average sports car weighs about 2,800 pounds, give or take a hundredweight, so there is a lot of mass moving down the road. But with all that mass, you still only have contact with the pavement in four small areas —the tire patches or the tiny spots where the rubber touches the pavement.

A lot of weight sits on each of these patches, so as you hum down the highway it is extremely important to know how each is working, individually as well as collectively. There is a chain: The tire is mounted to the rim, which, in turn, is bolted to the suspension, which is fastened to the frame, as is, for all practical purposes, the seat. And you, hopefully, are strapped to the seat.

Through this chain, you receive the handling inputs of the car—little signals that are constantly telling you how the tire patches are working. You must be sensitive to the car because it is giving you a lot of information. Don't isolate yourself from this information; feel what it is telling you, so you can react properly to make the car do what you want.

Learn to *feel* what the car is trying to tell you. Know, for example, when the left front tire is starting to slide, and learn what to do to correct this. The initial link in making the car do what you want it to do, is to feel it in the first place. There is mechanical input coming to you through different controls in the car, telling you if the particular areas they control are working properly. A good example of this is the brake pedal. You learn that by pushing the brake pedal down, say, one-and-a-half inches in a certain corner, the car slows down at a given rate. That rate becomes a sort of standard; so if you come into the next corner and you want to do the same thing, you push the pedal down an inch and a half and you expect the car to slow down at the same rate. If it doesn't slow down as quickly, you know that, for some reason, the brakes aren't working as well. The reason could be increased speed or the beginning of brake problems; but whatever the reason, it is a signal and you must learn to react quickly.

Signals can be audible. You can tell something's wrong by the squeal of the tires or the sound of the engine revs, so you must learn what everything sounds like when the car is working perfectly, otherwise you won't pick up the signal when it isn't working perfectly. You can learn to feel signals through the shift lever or through the seat. Sometimes the signals overlap. The inputs you feel through the steering column could be exactly the same ones you feel in the seat of your pants. The tire patch, for example, distorts when there is cornering force, so you must learn to detect improper distortion and react accordingly. Simply stated, you must know what it is you are feeling. So let's begin with the most basic maneuver to help you *feel* some of the things that are happening to the car—how to sit properly.

Seating

Since the seating position relates very closely to several important inputs, you should take advantage of these signals. A lot of them will come directly through the seat, so make sure you have your rear tucked well back in the seat. This will give you body contact with the area from which you receive these signals.

Adjust the seat so that you can operate the car in an efficient manner. The average driver probably sits too close to the wheel and if forced to make a quick maneuver, would undoubtedly get all tangled up in elbows and steering wheel. Sitting with your arms completely stretched out, locking your elbows, also gives you limited control—despite what a lot of Porsche drivers think. When your arms are fully extended, they become little more than levers to dial in the steering you want in either direction. You have very little feel of the wheel, and, worse than that, you are using only the muscles in your back, not any of the muscles in your arms. You might accomplish what you want for a few laps, but it is not likely to last because fatigue will set in quickly and your lap times will begin to show it. Your consistency will suffer as badly as your arms.

The ideal adjustment for seating is one where your arms are slightly bent, allowing you to use all the muscles in your back and arms. The same is true of the leg position. You should have the seat positioned so that you don't have to stretch and point your toes to get the pedals all the way down, and you should not be sitting with your knees poking through the spokes of the steering wheel. You need free and precise movement of your feet and legs.

You should always use the ball of the foot on the floor controls, so, as with the arms, you should have a slight bend in the knees when any of the controls are fully depressed. This way you can exert the exact pressure you want on any given control, at any given instant. Granted, there may have to be a compromise drawn between arm and leg angle because everybody isn't built with arms and legs of the specified length. Not even Recaro can build a seat to fit everybody. So if you must make a compromise between leg and arm position, slightly more emphasis should be placed on the arm position. If the arm position is right, you can probably live with a little stretch for the pedals. But if you can't depress any of them fully, you may have to resort to either building up the pedals or replacing the seat.

A good compromise usually can be made without too much difficulty and without too much modification. If you have a telescoping wheel, the problem can be solved perfectly, and if your car has a seat with a back angle adjustment and/or a height adjustment, you can find the one perfect seating position.

Some cars have a dead pedal, or at least a raised area to the left of the clutch. This is merely a place where you can brace your left foot when you are not using it for anything else. It will give you good support to hold you back in your seat. Use it.

Speaking of support, it should go without saying that seat belts are always to be worn. They are required on all race courses, but you should wear them at all times, required or not. All of the reasons you have ever heard for wearing seat belts are true. And, in addition to keeping you in a safer position during a crash, they keep you in the proper position during a high-speed turn—in front of the controls. Sudden, evasive moves on the highway could cause you to slide away from the proper seating position and leave you holding on to the wheel instead of controlling it. Seat belts help you operate the car more efficiently, so keep them buckled tightly. In a race car, they should be tight enough to actually hurt a little. Once the green flag is waved, you will not notice the discomfort. You *will* notice how well you stay directly in front of all the controls. The car should be an extension of your body, and that is not possible if you are rattling around inside of it.

Steering

Once you are seated properly in the car, your bucket well into the bucket seats, and tightly strapped in, the next thing you need to know is how to hold the steering wheel. Nobody has been able to explain why, but every driver's education class in America teaches that the wheel should be held with the hands in the 10 o'clock and 2 o'clock position. Close, but no cigar. A more sophisticated and far more effective method is to drop your hands to the 9 o'clock and 3 o'clock position. And, if you have spokes at those positions, hook your thumbs in them. If your wheel doesn't have spokes there, and you are a highly motivated driver, perhaps you should consider one of the many good racing-type steering wheels that are on the market.

With your hands gripping the wheel firmly—not white-knuckled, firmly —and your thumbs locked in, you can make a turn in either direction simply by dialing in the amount of steering you need. Seldom will you have to move your hands, which is good because you never want to be shuffling them about the wheel when you should be turning the car. Practice the proper technique. And watch how badly most street drivers handle a steering wheel.

Go down to the neighborhood shopping center, or anywhere, for that matter, where a 90-degree turn is required and observe how the average motorist starts the turn by swinging too wide, then, realizing the broad sweep the car is making, overcorrects, bringing it back in too far. Most drivers let the wheel spin freely through their hands until it gets to a place they think is right—but is usually wrong—and they grab it. The car goes

Bob Bondurant shows his students the proper way to hold a steering wheel.

zig-zagging down the road with the driver frantically trying to keep it between the double yellow lines and the row of parked cars on the right. Obviously, a high-speed turn requires a lot more precision and consistency. You should make the turn out of the shopping center fifty times and have it look as if there is one track. The steering wheel is a control you must use in a mechanical way if you want to get consistent results, and the only thing that should vary is the rate at which you move it.

If the turn is so sharp that it requires more than half a turn, there is a technique called a crossover, which will enable you to make a tight turn, using this basic technique:

You start out for a right-hand turn by bringing the right hand across and hooking the thumb under the left spoke. This should be done *before* you get to the turn. When you are ready to turn, start to pull the wheel across with your right hand, letting the wheel slide through your left hand until the right spoke comes around. Pick up the right spoke with your left hand and add any more steering needed. As you begin to come out of the corner, feed the wheel back, letting it again slide through your left hand, and smoothly bring your right hand back to the original 3 o'clock position. Lock your thumbs back into their respective positions. A tight left-hand turn is handled by moving your left hand to the opposite side, so, essentially, most of the work in a right turn is done by your right hand and most of the work in a left turn is done by your left hand. The crossover is another mechanical way to use the steering so you get the same results each time.

It is considered bad form to get into the middle of a corner and then realize you need more steering, particularly when you're in a pack of cars. The steering should have been accounted for *before* you got to the corner, and the crossover technique should have been started way back there.

Never start the first part of a turn by letting your hands meet at the top of the wheel and then try to negotiate the turn by pushing the wheel with one hand or the other. You should have already started to turn by then, so you've probably missed your proper turning point, and you'll look a lot like the little old man in the '61 Dodge, zig-zagging out of the parking lot.

Locking-in the thumbs (there is always at least one thumb hooked in) gives very positive control of the wheel and all but eliminates the possibility of the wheel being jerked out of your hands if a tire blows or you hit a hole —or another car.

It would take so much force to hold the wheel securely without hooking-in your thumbs that you would never be sensitive to the inputs, and your arms would tire quickly. There is one thing to remember, however: If your car is in a slide and it appears that the impact is going to straighten out the wheels from the outside, very quickly remove your thumbs from the spokes, because the sudden snap of the wheel could break them. Don't let go of the wheel, because there is always the outside chance that you might not hit whatever it is you are sliding toward, but do free your thumbs.

Being aware of the relationship of the steering wheel to the position of the front wheels is highly important. If you are not aware of exactly how much steering you have put in, you have no idea at all how much to take out to make the car do what's required. It is somewhat like flying an airplane when you can't see the horizon; the steering wheel could be a full turn farther than you think it is, and that could make an interesting difference in coming out of a corner. You must keep track of how far you have moved the wheel, particularly when correcting for a slide. With the scenery going in a different direction, it is often hard to remember how much steering you've put in, or in what direction for that matter; and a skid cannot be controlled properly if you don't know precisely what the front wheels are doing. Knowing where dead straight is with the wheels is a highly important consideration to high-performance driving. And the mechanical method of using the crossover makes it possible to remember what is happening to the front wheels. Unless you are driving a formula car, where you can simply look out and see the front wheels, the crossover method may be the only way to remember. It doesn't take that much practice to learn exactly where the wheels are pointing in any given situation.

For super-straight highway driving—Interstate 5, south of San Francisco, for example—where there may be no turns at all for many miles, following all of the racing techniques might get pretty boring. In fact, it may not be necessary to keep a constant feel for the car and to be tuned into the signals, because there won't be that many signals. So you may want to make a compromise here and there along the way, just to break the monotony. You can move your hands around and change your seating position or your leg position. But don't stray too far from the prescribed positions because you should always be aware of what is happening to the car in any given situation. Know what is happening around you, particularly to the other cars on the highway.

A winding, back road is a different story, and one more closely akin to the race track, as far as technique is concerned. There, it is not only important but a lot more fun—and a lot safer—to completely assume the racing configuration. Practice on the highway will help you perform better on the track, and learning the skills at 55 miles per hour or so will help to make you exact at that speed on the track. You can pick it up from there.

Shifting

Old County Road 606—or whatever your "dream road" may be—might also be a good spot to practice shifting. Sure, you've been shifting a car since you were knee-high to a Rover, but it is a thing a lot of people do incorrectly. Every time. The shift lever is probably the most abused control on the car. Many people take out their aggressions and anxieties on it. In any sort of speed event, you will find that a majority of the contestants feel that the faster you move the lever, or the more force you use on it, the faster you are going to get to the next corner. Wrong. Abusing the gearbox can put you out of the race before you get to the corner. The shift linkage and the gearbox itself are fairly delicate components and should be treated accordingly.

First you should determine how fast the linkage will work in order to get the car from one gear to the next. Once you have determined that, don't try to move it any quicker. Guide it in at that speed, no faster and no slower, and be gentle with it.

Most people grab the shift lever with their fist and yank it this way and that, unconsciously abusing it. There are some who shift with such force that you can see the entire upper part of their body move with the shift lever. Stand near the corner of any road course and observe how many drivers rock back and forth as they shift gears. They are slamming that rascal right in there. And they are doing it wrong.

The best way to break an aggressive shifting habit is to learn how to hold the lever in the first place. It's simple. Rest your hand on top of it, with the palm opened on the ball of the lever, your hand completely relaxed. Resting there in that position, you can more accurately read the inputs coming through the lever to the sensitive portion of your hand. And, even if you wanted to, you could not exert a lot of force on the lever. It's impossible. So, with your hand resting on top, simply cup it and guide the lever back from first to second with your fingertips. Then open your hand and guide it forward into third with the heel of your hand. On cars that are a little harder to shift, this method is particularly effective. It allows you to feel exactly what is happening in the gearbox, and you can refine your technique to the point that it actually goes into gear easier. Just as important, you can quickly feel any changes that are taking place in the gearbox and make any necessary adjustments or changes before it fails.

Once you have mastered the shifting technique, you should begin practice on the heel-and-toe method of downshifting. Heel-and-toe is something everybody talks about but few do properly. Its function is simple: It is a technique used to brake the car and downshift smoothly at the same time. Nothing more. It matches the engine speed in a selected lower gear to the rear end speed, and that, in itself, makes the car shift easier. While all this is happening, you are slowing down. It's not magic, but if done properly, you'll think it is. Failure to use the heel-and-toe method can upset the balance on various parts of the car, and could cause wheels to lock up or the car to slide or any number of sticky situations.

Heel-and-toe downshifting is a complicated maneuver at first because there are a lot of things to remember and many things are happening almost together. If you have trouble with walking and chewing gum at the same time, you are likely to take a little longer learning the heel-and-toe technique. But most people will pick it up quickly.

You must double-clutch because it is necessary to use all three pedals, which is interesting since you have but two feet. Double-clutching actually makes the procedure easier.

Contrary to popular belief, downshifting is not used for slowing down the car with the help of the engine any more than double-clutching is used to make it all sound good—that extra zap of the engine thrown in there. It all has a purpose. The prime object of downshifting is to get the car into the proper gear so that you have the required power to exit a corner. If it becomes necessary to shift from third to second, for instance, you certainly don't want to take your foot off the brake and put it on the accelerator to bring up the revs—which, incidentally, is absolutely necessary to make a smooth downshift—and then put your foot back on the brake. All this would take away from your braking, which, in turn, would take away your ability to make the corner—something you probably wanted very badly to do. So what you do is brake with the ball of your right foot and use the side or heel of the same foot to press on the accelerator to bring up the revs as you come down through the gears. Hang in there; it works. You are braking, and you are matching the engine speed with the rear axle speed. You are getting a smooth downshift. All of this is done *before* you get to the corner. Before the turning starts.

Here's how it's done: With your left foot resting on the dead pedal and your right foot on the accelerator, bring your right foot over and start squeezing on the brakes, *keeping your heel off the floor!* Put your left foot on the clutch and depress it. Pull the shift lever into neutral and let out the clutch, then start to roll the side of your left foot or your heel (whichever is easier for you) over on the throttle. Roll up the revs slightly and push in the clutch again. Move the shift lever from neutral into the next lower gear while the revs are up. Let out the clutch as you are rolling off the accelerator so that the revs are just starting to fall, matching up everything.

It sounds complicated, but it is a maneuver that can be practiced anywhere. And should be. Start by sitting in your car with the engine running, and roll your foot over on the gas, always keeping the ball of your foot on the brake. Do that part until you can do it smoothly, then move to the highway. Practice this technique while driving to work, at every traffic light, and at every tight corner. Practice until the whole sequence of events becomes second nature. Then you can try it at speed.

Heel-and-toe is vital, because without it you will never master the art of smoothly and efficiently downshifting and slowing down at the same time.

Oversteer and Understeer

By now you should have some feel for the mechanical side of high-performance driving, but none of the techniques matters a great deal if you don't know the handling characteristics of the car itself. Does it understeer or oversteer?

Understeer, to one extent or another, is a loss of adhesion at one or both of the front wheels. So, very simply, it is a front wheel skid. The car wants to continue in a straight line, but the rear tires are actually taking over more of the car's steering; they are pointed straight and they are trying to make the car go straight, even though you might wish very much to make it turn. A 100 percent understeer situation occurs when you have the steering wheel locked in either direction but the car is moving straight ahead. Pushing or plowing are also terms for the same condition.

The cause of understeer is usually quite simple—too much speed in a corner. There are, however, some cars that have an inherent tendency to understeer; the forces to make them want to go straight have overcome the forces at the front tires. Understeering is usually dictated by weight distribution, as in the case of a front-engined car.

A good analogy to understeer is the flight of a dart. A dart has a heavy front end and a light rear end, and it reaches the target in the front-end-first attitude, regardless of how you throw it. If you throw it backwards, it turns over in midair; the heavy end turns toward the direction of flight. It is one of Newton's basic laws of physics: The heavy end of any object wants to go first. So the placement of an engine has a big effect on how the car is going to react at speed in turns. The densest end—the one with the engine —always has a tendency to keep going straight. You may not be aware of this at all times, but it does. You can overcome this tendency by using the controls correctly. You can move the weight, and you can add to or subtract from the amount of the skid.

It is very important that you realize how your car's weight is distributed when it is sitting still, and how your use of the controls—brake, throttle, steering—is going to *change* the weight distribution, by moving it forward or backward, to make it work better at one end or not as well at the other.

How do wet conditions or front-wheel drive affect understeer? Wet pavement accentuates the situation and front-wheel drive does little, if anything, to correct it. It is a complete fairy tale that a front-wheel drive car will pull you around a corner. Unfortunately, it gives the impression of doing just that, until you get close to the limit. But when it reaches the limit, front-wheel drive understeers exactly the same as a rear-wheel drive, front-engined car. The problem, of course, is that you are probably in over your head by this point.

Hard braking—or any braking, for that matter—only stops the tires and wheels; so if you slam on your brakes so hard in an understeer condition that you lock up the wheels, you might just as well toss the steering wheel out the window. It is no longer of any use to you at all. You are in a 100 percent understeer situation, and you can spin the wheel in either direction with no effect whatsoever on your forward course.

Understeer can occur on the highway or the race track, in a high-speed turn or in a drastic evasive maneuver to miss an object that is suddenly in your path. It is exactly the same as being on solid ice. And the first thing most people do is get on the brakes, hard. You only have to try that once to know it is a mistake.

In understeer conditions the car is actually very stable. The only signal you get is a little limp feeling in the steering wheel. The car is sliding along, and you realize that it is not stopping as quickly as you want it to. You see the right lane is open, so you turn the car in that direction to drive around the problem. Surprise. The car, with wheels locked up and the steering wheel turned, slides right into the object you had so hoped to miss. Next time you see a rear-ender, look at the front wheels of the car that did the hitting. In practically every case the wheels will be turned either sharply right or sharply left. But it hit the other car just the same.

You can figure it out then. The most important thing to be aware of in an understeer situation is the status of your front wheels. Are they locked up? If they are, the solution is quite simple: Get off the brake pedal. Unfortunately, it is not always that easy. It is an unnatural reaction to get *off* the brakes to avoid hitting an object. Getting out of other types of skids is fairly instinctive, but not so for the front-wheel skid. For one thing, in this kind of skid, the front brakes work even better than normal because more weight has been shifted forward, making braking a critical factor.

Front brakes are designed to be more effective than rear brakes—perhaps as much as 80 percent front to 20 percent rear—otherwise the rear would always lock up as the weight moves forward in a braking situation, as it always does. So what do you do first? Well, you certainly don't brake. You get off the accelerator. Then you brake. Easily. By doing these two things, in this order, you move the weight forward to give the front tire patches more adhesion. Decreasing the speed starts to eliminate the cause of the skid in the first place, so, therefore, it makes a great deal of sense to back off the gas. Accelerating would move the weight back and further reduce the effectiveness of the front tire patches.

By getting the weight on the front end of the car, you have increased the adhesion *and* you have created a situation where gentle braking can further slow down the car. By reducing the speed you have also reduced the tendency of total forward motion, and, unless you have grossly overestimated the situation, the car should track right around the corner. But if you brake too hard, the wheels will lock up and you will have made the situation even worse.

The normal response to the question of what to do in case of a skid is, "Turn into it," but this has nothing whatsoever to do with a front-wheel skid. It's just that most people tend to think of all skids as being *rear-*wheel skids, because the front-wheel skid is usually far more forgiving. A lot of people get out of the latter without even knowing they have been in one. Simply by letting up on the gas, they eliminate the cause of the skid. When they don't get out of one, they have no idea at all why they rear-ended the guy, and why the car didn't respond to the steering they had put into the car to avoid the accident.

If you took your brand-new XJS Jaguar and whizzed down an off ramp and the car started to understeer about halfway down, you would probably back off the gas a little and the car would track right on down the ramp. If somebody asked you at the bottom, "Were you in a skid?" you might respond, "Hell, no, I just paid thirty thousand dollars for this car and it doesn't *skid.* " It would be a typical response, because most skids of this type are minimal, and the average driver would have no idea he had even been in a skid. As a rule, you only know it if the wheels are locked up, as on ice, and then everything is exaggerated.

This bears repeating: If you have locked up the front wheels, simply unlock them. By getting off the brakes. It is a maneuver much easier said than done, because if you have them locked up, you had a definite desire to slow down in the first place, so it is going to be very difficult to get that right foot off the brake pedal; but unless you do, you can try anything else you want—scream, pray, turn the wheel right, turn it left, anything—it's not going to make any difference. You must get the front wheels turning again.

Unfortunately, this is one aspect of car control that you can't practice all that much. About the best you can hope for is to learn to distinguish the

A student at the Bondurant School of High Performance Driving puts a Datsun Z through its paces.

feel of a front-wheel skid and to feel the difference it makes simply by getting the front wheels rolling again; or the difference a simple move like letting up on the gas makes. It is something that you need to experience a few times. After that, it quickly becomes a natural reaction.

Even though you might not want to induce an understeer situation, at least learn to recognize one. If you go into a turn and, after braking, you feel a limpness in the steering wheel, get off the gas and ease off on the brakes until the limpness in the wheel goes away. That tells you the wheels are turning again. You could straighten the wheels—that's a sure-fire way to correct understeer—but you would go right off the road or track, and that's not exactly what you want to do. It's a lot like aquaplaning or driving on ice; you don't want to do *anything* drastic.

If, after backing off and easing off the brakes, the car still isn't coming around fast enough, then you can try turning into the skid; but there's no use trying it sooner, because it won't work until the car has at least started to turn. By causing the skid to be wider, it might help you get through the corner—unless you're trying to make a 15-mile-per-hour corner at 80 miles per hour.

Oversteer, as you may have guessed by now, is a rear-wheel skid. In this case, the car is steering *too* much. Oversteer is often caused by spinning rear tires—overacceleration or slippery pavement. Or it may be the result of locking the rear wheels, or merely of the fact that it is a rear-engined car, which means an inherently oversteering one. Or the most frequent cause—too much speed in the corner. All of these conditions shift the weight to the rear end and, instead of the car wanting to plow right on through, nose-end first, the rear end wants to go first, so around it comes.

Exactly the same things that cause understeer cause oversteer; one merely relates to the back end and one to the front end. But with understeer, the car is very stable; it just wants to go straight. Oversteer is the exact opposite. The car won't go straight at all; it just wants to spin, so it is very *un*stable.

When you find yourself going a little too fast in a corner, and you feel the back end starting to let go, do exactly what your grandfather told you to do in a slide—turn into the direction of the slide. But first, back off the throttle and don't come down on the brakes.

On an oval track, if the rear end slides, it slides to the right, so the drivers turn to the right, or toward the wall. If it goes around too far and the driver can tell he's not going to catch it, he waits until it gets around and then you immediately see a lot of smoke from the tires. He has purposely locked up the wheels. If he had continued trying to catch it, he would be right up into the wall, so he stands on the brakes, locks up all four wheels, and this tends to make him go straight, except that he's on a banked track, so the centrifugal force pulls him down into the infield, which is where he wants to be.

Spins don't always happen to *you*. It is possible for the other guy to spin, so you must know what to do if a car spins in front of you. There are certain things that work. Sometimes. In most cases, a spinning car will spin to the inside of the corner rather than to the outside, so it usually isn't too good an idea to try to go underneath a spinning car. For one thing, you are probably at maximum in your turning arc, so if you tighten up your line to drive underneath him, you will probably spin, too. If you turn to the outside, the car will go there easily because of centrifugal force; but, since this is not your proper line, it could cause a spin in that direction. What's left? Only one thing: Steer right for him. The chances of him being right there when you get to that point are slim. He's going to be on one side or the other. You have a much better chance of missing him, and since you haven't altered your line drastically, you've minimized the chance of spinning your own car.

Cornering

Any time you come to a point where you have to slow down, you must initiate the change very smoothly. You never jump on the brake; you *squeeze* the brake. The brakes, like any other control on the car, should be used like rheostats instead of On and Off switches. In other words, you dial in more and more intensely, and you dial out less and less intensely.

In braking for a corner, squeeze on the brakes; take a car length or two to gradually come down hard on them. This squats the car down and gradually moves the weight forward. You can't stop the weight from moving forward, but you can *initiate* it at the proper time, and you can *control* its movement. For the most part.

Hard braking is done in a straight line, because the most efficient way to slow down a car is to do it as hard as possible without locking up the wheels, and this can only be done in a straight line. Maximum speed is taken off in the straight, right up to the point where you begin to make your arc for the corner. This point is called the turndown point. Obvious.

A lot of people will tell you that after you start turning, you can't use your brakes; some instructors even tell you never to brake in a corner. Don't listen. For one thing, the brakes can do something beside stop the car, or slow it down. Look at it this way: If you come in fast and squeeze on the brakes, the weight moves to the front of the car. If you don't use the brakes in the corner—say you just get to the turndown point and hop off the brakes —well, the weight will come off the front end and go back to the rear. It would unload the front wheels, and the most important thing you are trying to do at this point is to get the car turned. Plain and simple. You are turning with the front tires, so why take the weight off them and cause understeer?

In skiing, you learn that by leaning forward and putting weight on the ski tips, you can carve turns beautifully. You can do the same thing with brakes by keeping the car leaning forward. So stay on the brakes a little and keep the weight on the front two tire patches, and the car will carve a turn. The important words here, of course, are "a little." If you were to stay on the brakes as hard as when going straight, before the turn, the weight would continue going forward with the same force and, as the car turned, the weight would shift across to the outside front wheel. The inside front wheel, being unloaded all of a sudden, would lock up, and a locked-up wheel loses adhesion. That is why many people are reluctant to brake at all in a corner.

But try this: As you feed in the steering to make the turn, and as the weight is shifted across to the outside of the car, ride or trail off the brakes, keeping as much weight forward as possible, but not enough to lock up the inside front wheel. Ideally, you should proportion the cornering force with the braking force in the first one-third of the corner. You will keep the weight on the corner of the car where it is necessary.

When you get into the line technique for the corner, you will find that often it is necessary to sacrifice some speed going into a corner, so you can get the car pointed properly coming out. A good rule of thumb is to trail the brakes during the first third of the corner. By then you should have finished turning in and can begin to trail off the brakes as you start to open up on your steering. You will have trailed off the brakes completely and be back on the gas when you need it—when the car comes out long and wide. You can squeeze on the gas a little harder or more abruptly than you can squeeze on the brakes—unless you're driving an 800-horsepower Can-Am car.

The point where you stop turning in and begin to open up on the steering is known as the apex of the turn, and the point where you reach the outside edge of the track, when you have completely finished the turn, is the exit point. If you find you've reached an improper exit point—where you must tighten up more on the steering or open up a lot—you have turned down at the wrong point. It probably means you misjudged the braking on entering the turn.

You will notice in Diagram 1, which illustrates a hypothetical corner, that there are two lines going through it, a dotted one and a solid one. Both lines start at the outside edge of the road and finish at the outside edge of the road, although not at the same points. Somewhere near the middle of the turn, they clip the inside edge of the road, again at a different point. No matter where that point is, it is called the clipping point, or the apex of the turn.

There is probably no single word in all of sports car racing that is as widely used or as misunderstood as the *apex.* You will find about as many different apexes to a turn as you have drivers. You can put it anywhere, but

1. HOW TO CORNER PROPERLY

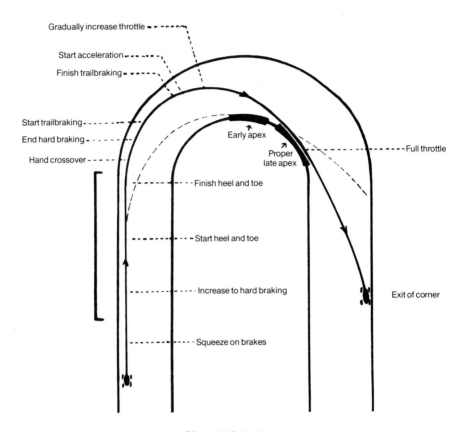

it is always the point where you stop turning in and begin to open up on the steering to begin the exit.

If you are trying to go through a corner quickly and safely, anything you can do to make it less of a corner will improve the situation. So you are basically always trying to straighten out a corner. You will note that both lines in the diagram have less of an arc than the corner itself. You might guess that one of them is right and the other is somewhat less desirable. Let's examine both.

The dotted line has its apex sooner in the corner, so it is referred to as an early apex. It is a constant arc radius through the corner, so the apex is right in the middle. Let's say that a car can go through the corner at 80 miles per hour without spinning. In other words, that's the point where understeer and oversteer are equal—assuming that you haven't braked too hard or the gal in the red tank top you were using as a turndown marker hasn't moved. If you were to increase the speed to even 82 miles per hour, the arc would become greater, because the centrifugal force would automatically increase the radius, and you would use more road coming out of the turn—which is racer talk for either getting into the wall or off the track.

You've probably already seen the problem with the early apex line through the corner. There is no more road to *use* coming out. You simply can't allow the radius to increase because there isn't any place to go. Safely. You must maintain that speed all the way through, and not accelerate until you have completely exited the corner and have gotten the car straightened out.

Now, let's look at the solid, or late apex, line through the same corner. The car has been driven farther into the turn going in before starting to turn. Because of this, the turn has to be much sharper than the one indicated by the dotted line, so the car must be slowed down to, say, 78 miles per hour. But, as it gets deeper into the turn, the arc begins to straighten out much earlier, allowing the driver to increase the speed a lot sooner.

The exit speed, consequently, is probably 5 mph greater than that of the dotted line or early apex line. The driver has done most of the angling and turning of the car in the first one-third of the corner; so as he clips the apex at the inside of the track, he has already begun to open up on the steering and to start rolling back on the throttle. Rolling down on the gas is much more comfortable than either coasting or braking. You will spend a lot more time rolling down on the throttle if you follow the later apex line than if you take the dotted-line approach.

The main advantage to the later apex, of course, is that you gain more speed coming out than you lose going in. We mentioned earlier that you might have to sacrifice at one point, but that the sacrifice would more than make up for itself later on. This is the point. Exit speed is the most important aspect, if you're trying to go fast through a corner. Obviously, this is affected greatly by your entrance into a turn. Even if you lose 5 mph going in and pick up 5 coming out, you're better off, so don't make that demon dive into the corner. Sacrifice a little there, get the car set up properly, clip the late apex, and accelerate like mad coming out.

The dotted-line approach means you have to be slowed down to 80 mph much sooner, which gives the solid line a longer straight-line braking area. It means that the solid-line car can go maybe 120 mph for a longer period coming in. Everything about it is better.

Let's look at the same diagram from a different perspective, reversing the flow of traffic: The solid line becomes an early apex, and the driver has to tighten up on the steering and slow down coming out, otherwise he would be off somewhere about the porta-potties. It's not all that unusual. Many drivers get deep into a turn and suddenly realize they have to tighten up on the steering; so they dial in that extra amount needed to keep them on the track but fail to back off the necessary amount on the gas. They have too much speed for the corner and, since most cars are front-engined and inherently understeering, they go right off the outside of the track, wheels turned and all. The Porsches go into an oversteer and the rear of the car spins.

The point, of course, is that no matter which way you look at the diagram, you should never have to make drastic changes in the steering in the last two-thirds of the turn. You should be opening up smoothly, never tightening up on the steering. Leave that to the guy who made the early apex and who is now walking the tightrope between the edge of the track and whatever is immediately beyond that.

If you find yourself still turning in for the corner when you are more than halfway through it, you have done something wrong. You probably turned in too early, clipped too early an apex, and you're having to fight for it by keeping the steering held in too tightly, for too long. If you can't start to open up on the steering and start to roll down on the gas by the time you get to the apex, your apex is too early.

It will help if you can pick out a nice *legal* spot—a shopping center on weekends, *with* permission, for example—and mark off a corner with pylons or plastic milk jugs or anything that it won't hurt to run over. The first thing you should do is determine the proper apex, one that will enable you to get your turning completed by the first one-third of the turn and will enable you to open up on the steering as you go past it. On the race course, you will have to find your own marker—a break in the pavement, a patch of newer asphalt, whatever—but make sure it's something that will not move.

Once you've determined the location of the proper late apex (see Diagram 2) for your turn, practice until your entrance, your clipping point, and your

2. 90° TURN

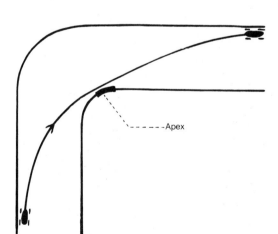

exit are letter perfect. Start slowly and increase your speed only when you are confident and smooth at the slower speed. Now, combine the line technique with the straight-line braking, the heel-and-toe downshifting, and the crossover grip for a smooth and consistent cornering technique.

An important consideration: All of the above can be applied to the highway. Your technique may have to be modified somewhat when you come to blind turns but, regardless of the location, road or track, the driver with the later apex is in a better position for the corner and for anything that might be happening there.

In this position, you can see the corner sooner and you will be going slower when you see it. As a result, you will have a lot more room to correct for problems. If you could drive around a whole race course with your foot to the floor, you would have incredible lap times, but since that's completely impossible, it boils down to this: The driver who spends *more* time with his foot on the throttle is the guy who will go quicker—everything else being equal. That applies perfectly to the late apex technique.

Now that we've created a beautiful racing hero bubble, where everything can be explained by a late apex, it's time to burst that bubble.

Not all corners are simple radius corners like the one in Diagram 2. Sad, but true. There are all sorts of interesting things to make the life of the sports car driver a complex one; little things like varying radius turns—diminishing and increasing radius—elevation changes—uphill and downhill—esses, and, at times, combinations thereof. But don't give up now. You've come too far.

Examine Diagram 3, which gives an example of a diminishing radius turn, Diagram 4, which shows an increasing radius turn, and Diagram 5,

3. DIMINISHING RADIUS TURN   **4. INCREASING RADIUS TURN**

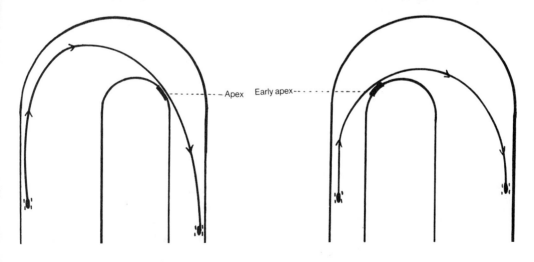

Apex   Early apex

showing an "S" turn. It's not as tough to remember as you might imagine.

You really have no choice in the diminishing radius turn (Diagram 3) because you have a wide road going into a narrow one. You simply don't have any road to spare coming out of the corner, so you have to have your turn completed by the time you've reached your apex. If any change is made at all, you would probably want to make the apex even later.

The increasing radius turn (Diagram 4) is just as easily rationalized. It is one of the few exceptions to the late apex rule. It is a time when an early apex should be used. You will note that in the increasing radius turn you have a narrow road going into a wider one, so why bother sacrificing anything going *into* the turn if there is a whole bunch of road to use coming *out?* You can use an early apex and let the car drift out much wider coming out, still opening up on the steering and getting on the gas as if it were a late apex exit. This is an ideal sort of turn because you don't lose as much going in *or* coming out. A late apex on this type of turn would simply cost you time. Conversely, an early apex on a diminishing radius turn could be very serious.

The late apex is still best with an "S" turn (Diagram 5) because you have to be concerned with exactly the same things as you were in Diagram 1: braking, turning, and getting the car lined up. Make a very late apex in the first part of the "S," in order to make a semi-late one in the second part. You turn more in the first one to get the car lined up in the second one.

Here's a rule to keep in mind: Always set up a late apex until you know what the road does coming out of the turn. You can modify it later, but always move the apex *back.* Don't ever start with an early apex and move it forward. If you start with it too far forward and move it back, as in the case of the increasing radius turn, you will lose a little time. But if you're going fast and you've set it up too early, you may not get another chance to move it forward.

A good example of this can be found on the majority of freeway entrance ramps. Most get tighter or narrower as you get closer to the main highway. So if you stay out wider at the beginning and clip a late apex, you will have all your turning done by the time you reach the highway, and you can merge into traffic much more easily going in a straighter line.

Diagram 1 puts together on one chart everything you've been told thus far—squeezing on the brakes; heel-and-toe downshift; hard, straight-line braking; crossover grip; turndown point for the late apex turn; trailbraking; and the proper exit. It should serve as a reminder of all the aspects of high-performance cornering. It is the exact technique taught at the Bondurant School of High Performance Driving. So, if you are having trouble picking it up, or in putting any of it together, you might want to consider a school such as this. As was discussed earlier, the Bondurant School has some distinct advantages over some of the others, but it certainly doesn't

5. S-TURN

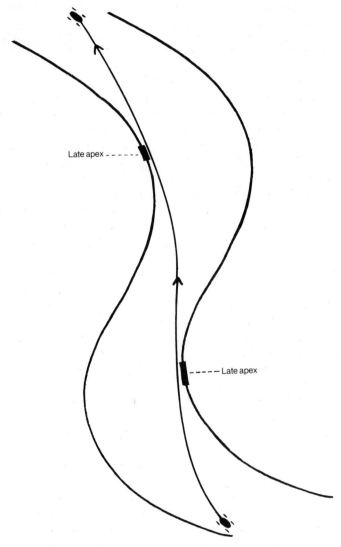

Late apex ------

----- Late apex

rule out any of the top five or six. A lot of them can make your trip to the winner's circle a quicker one.

Controlling the Slide

Racers are filled with wisdom. They talk about slides and crashes with total abandon. To the statement, "It is better to hit something going back-

wards than forwards," one driver recently added, "Sure, you can't see it."
It is, in fact, better to hit it backwards, but there is another explanation: You
have more support in your seat during that type of crash.

The point is that slides *can* be controlled, in direct proportion, of course,
to the experience of the driver. At the Bondurant School, students drive on
the skid pad during the very first day of instruction; that's how important
they consider slide control. They want the students to learn immediately
how it feels to spin in a car, and to see how easily a spin can be corrected,
if you catch it in time—and what to do if you don't catch it. All of this is
designed to teach you how to avoid a crash.

The obvious and ultimate answer to the slide is to simply go to a good
school; but if that is impractical, you might want to think about setting up
your own skid pad. This is a somewhat complicated process, so you will
need some help. It would be a good club project. For one thing, you will
need help in corraling the curious onlookers.

Finding the proper spot will be your most difficult task. Most shopping
center store owners would be sore wrought on a Monday morning to find
their parking lot covered with oil, or perhaps to find an MG in their sales
room. But if you can get permission from someone who has a large parking
lot that is not in use on weekends, you can wet it down with a water soluble
oil. This should work nicely, provided there is an adequate water supply to
clean up the whole mess after you've finished with it.

You don't need to oil the entire lot. A patch near the center, about 100
feet long by 50 feet wide, will work nicely.

Spraying the area with water will also work, and it eliminates the bothersome clean-up. A perfectly dry surface works, too, but it's a little harder
on the equipment and a whole lot noisier. And an oiled surface gives much
better results at lower speeds. The car reacts in a 30-mph spin on oil with
about the same response as a 60-mph dry surface spin. The oiled track will
not draw as many onlookers because of the quiet action on the skid pad.

Whatever surface you choose, make sure you have plenty of room beyond
the skid area to stop, and at least a 100-foot area on either side to accommodate some of the wild spins before you get the hang of it. Each end of
the pad should have about 250 feet (more if possible) for speed buildup
and runout, since you will be approaching from and stopping at either
end.

Rule Number One: You don't have to worry about rolling over, because
a spinning car has no traction—that's why it's spinning, in the first place
—and without traction, you can't roll over. Simple.

Rule Number Two: You must know how many turns, lock to lock, your
steering has. So, with the car sitting still, slowly crank the wheel in either
direction until it stops. Remember this information, because you'll need it
later.

The author gets ready to "go racing" at the Bondurant School.

End of rules. That's all you need to know to start. Everything else just works—take my word for it. And now you're ready to start.

Since you have no way to induce a front-wheel lock-up, you'll have to settle for a four-wheel lock-up, which gives roughly the same reaction.

Besides, the rear brakes don't work that well anyway. For rear-wheel lock-up, you can rely on your emergency brake.

Start by learning the feel of a front wheel lock-up. Approach the skid area (let's assume it is oiled) at about 30 mph. As soon as all four wheels are on the skid pad, lock up the wheels with the foot brake. You will feel a very light—limp, as they say—steering wheel. This indicates that the wheels are not turning. When they are turning, there is always a little bit of runout or vibration. So you can tell if the wheels have stopped turning simply by the lack of vibration. And by the light feel of the wheel.

You are in a 100 percent understeer condition. The caster is not going to work for you any more because the front wheels aren't turning. Normally, if you're driving down the street and you make a turn and release the wheel, it will straighten out by itself. But that's not going to work. It's like a gyroscope: When the wheels stop turning, there's no longer any effect. That's why you have to remember the straight-ahead position on the steering wheel. The car is no longer going to do it for you.

After you have made a couple of runs, feeling the lightness of the steering wheel when the front wheels are locked up, try turning the wheel in either direction while skidding. Nothing happens. Interesting. The car slides straight ahead, no matter how little or how much steering you put in. It is a perfect exercise to see whether you can still find straight ahead. If the car goes straight when you ease off the brakes and get the front wheels turning again, you have done your job well. If it goes off at some odd angle, see how much steering is needed to correct it. You should practice this until the car goes straight every time. You will have to figure out your own technique —the one that works best for you—because of the great variety of reference points on various steering wheels.

You have felt the car in a front-wheel lock-up, and, once you have mastered finding straight ahead on the wheel and are certain you know the feel of understeer (the front-wheel skid), you should begin work on the rear-wheel spin—oversteer. Approach the pad at the same speed as before, only this time, when you hit the oil, lock up the rear wheels by pulling or stepping—whichever is appropriate—on the emergency brake. Let the car spin around once to get the feeling. Check again to make sure there is nothing on either side to slide into.

On the next pass through, lock up the rear brakes once more. This time, as the rear end starts around, let up on the brakes and steer into the slide. Try to stop it before it loops. If you do catch it, be ready to correct again as the rear end comes back, making sure it doesn't go too far and spin the other way. Practice this maneuver until you can stop the spin every time. It certainly helps if you have someone else in the car with you. That person can initiate the brake lock-ups, and can do it in such a way as to take you by surprise—the way it will happen on a race track. When you become proficient, your helper can add a lock-up just about the time you get it all put together from the previous spin. It is good practice.

You have felt the two types of handling characteristics in operation— understeer and oversteer—and, by now, you should know how to correct for them. But you must also know what to do if you *can't* stop the car from spinning, which is often the case on the race track. Not all slides can be stopped, and there will be times when you might *choose* to slide, perish the thought, to avoid an accident. Either way, you will want to initiate a few slides so that you can learn to use them as an evasive action, or simply to learn *control* of the race car.

The first slide to initiate is the forward 180 or, as they like to call it in NASCAR, the "bootleg turn." It's done like this:

Enter the pad on the extreme right side (or left—it doesn't really matter as long as you give yourself the entire width of the pad in which to slide) at about 30 miles per hour. When all four wheels are on the pad, turn the wheel about one-quarter turn to the left—no more, one-quarter of a turn —and, as the car starts to turn, pull the emergency brake hard to lock up the rear wheels. As the rear end begins to swing around, release the brake, return the steering wheel to straight ahead, and kick the car out of gear. It isn't necessary to put the car into neutral to complete the slide, but it will prevent engine stall when the spin is over—which is highly desirable if you're left sitting in the middle of a race course.

Now, here is the hard part: Hold the steering wheel in the straight-ahead position. You will be inclined to start trying to correct for the slide as the rear end comes around more and more, but under no circumstance should you move the wheel. If you hold it in the straight-ahead position, the car will spin around to 180 degrees and roll straight backwards. It will stop spinning at 180 degrees. And it will do it every time if you return the wheel to straight ahead and *hold it there*. Once the car is rolling straight back, squeeze on the brakes and bring it to a gradual stop. Jumping on the brakes at this point will cause the car to spin again.

The whole maneuver works even better on dry pavement. The more traction you get, the better it works; it's just that the oiled surface allows you to experience the feel of a high-speed spin at a much slower speed, which is desirable when you are just starting.

The obvious advantage of the forward 180 is in controlling the duration or arc of the spin. If you go roaring into a turn and find that you're over your head and are not going to be able to catch the slide by turning into it, and—for the sake of your sponsor, if nothing else—you would like to regain control as quickly as possible, get off the brakes, return the wheel to straight ahead, and wait for the 180. *Then* gradually stop the car. You will find that you have covered far less of the track than if you had simply let the spin take its course. It probably wouldn't have stopped at 180. If you've gotten it out of gear, the engine will still be running, and you can pop it back in and go merrily on your way, looking pretty professional for someone who has just lost it. You will be surprised, but the getting-the-car-in-neutral part will come automatically. The rest will take practice.

Remembering that you will want to *stop* more slides than start them, it might be wise to go back at this point and practice catching the slide again. You will still miss enough of them so that you can work on the bootleg turn from time to time. After all, it is the perfect combination: Try to catch the slide, but if you can't, try to control its duration.

Think about what you are going to do: To stop a rear-wheel skid, turn the steering wheel in the direction you want the car to go. It might not be where you had planned to go originally, but you must first regain control before you can go in the proper direction again. By turning in the direction you want the car to go initially, you are turning into the slide. It may be an easier way to remember what to do. And if you have to think about it on the track, it's probably already too late.

To stop a front-wheel slide, get off the gas and ease off the brakes.

Here's another interesting fact about slides: As the car turns sideways on a dry race track, it will stick better. You will have a lot of friction working for you, and you will have more time to catch it than you will on a skid pad, where, without the friction, the car will slide farther and faster.

You will have to use a lot more steering to correct for a slide on a skid pad; that's why the race track will be duck soup once you have mastered the pad.

It is important to try and correct properly the first time a car slides, because a slide back the other way is tougher to correct than the first one. For one thing, you've already turned the wheel one way or the other, and to correct for the second slide you will have to turn the wheel back twice as far. This will take longer, and the car won't be likely to wait for you to catch up.

They tell the story in NASCAR about the late Joe Weatherly at Darlington a few years ago. Weatherly had come out of the fourth turn sideways. The rear end of his car swung to the right, then left, and right again. It zig-zagged all the way down the front straightaway, with Weatherly trying desperately to "gather it up." But Weatherly couldn't get it under control, and crashed into the wall going into the second turn. Uninjured, except for his pride, he climbed out of the car and strode back toward the pits. A NASCAR official rushed up and yelped, "What happened, Joe?" Weatherly didn't even break stride. "Got a lil' behind on my steerin'," he replied.

It has happened to all of us.

It's the second spin you have to learn to get rid of, and the best place to do it is on the skid pad. You must learn to correct for the first slide so that you don't go into a second one. The only way you can do that is to anticipate a second slide. It is exactly like what you were told to do when approaching a spot on the race track that appears to be slippery: You approach it with caution, and you expect the car to slide, therefore you're right on top of it if it does. So, if you anticipate the second slide, you're already a step ahead of the car. Forget apexes and everything else at that moment. They don't matter any longer. Just remember, when you feel the rear end go out and you know that the angle has stopped increasing—the car has sort of taken a bite—you've stopped the slide. You also know that it's going to come back; you've fed in the proper factors to make it do just that. So, as soon as you feel it get that bite, start turning the wheel in the opposite direction to correct for the second slide before it happens. What you are actually doing is driving the front end over to where the rear end is going to go. More importantly, you are keeping the car straight. Second, third, and fourth slides are caused by turning the wheel too slowly or by overcorrecting on the first and subsequent slides—getting a little behind on your steering.

The next spin to master is the reverse 180, which, even if you never use it anyplace else, is great for getting out of your driveway. In the reverse spin, you have, in effect, rear-wheel steering, so all you have to do is crank the wheel around the way you want the car to slide, and it will come around. This is something like steering a boat.

As you approach the skid pad in reverse, you must be heading in a straight line. When you're on the pad, get off the gas, turn the wheel hard right or left, either way (left if you want to spin left, and vice versa). Now comes the hard part: *Hold the wheel in that position.* This is absolutely the most unnatural thing you will ever do in a car. On a skid pad. The instant the rear end starts around, kick it out of gear; you will want to start opening up on the steering, but if you do, the car will spin all over the pad. If you hold the steering in until the spinning car comes around, you'll find that it will catch at 180 degrees, and then you can open up on the steering and head right down the pad. You will look sensational.

This technique will work perfectly every time, but you have to turn the wheel quickly. The faster you turn the wheel (at least half a turn), the smaller the arc will be. If you turn the wheel just a little, you'll end up in a big sweeping slide, using up a lot of the road.

The reverse 180 is a maneuver they stress in both the high-performance classes and the antiterrorist, antikidnapping course at the Bondurant School. One way to remember which way to turn the wheel is this: If you turn the car initially toward the thing you want to avoid, you will eventually spin away from it; if something is on the left, turn the wheel right. This works on road or track, and is particularly exciting when linked with a forward 180 to produce a 360-degree spin.

There aren't many times when space permits a 360-degree spin on a race track, but you should know how to do it, just in case you ever get the chance. It is the only time you can spin a car and still look terrific.

There are two types of 360-degree spins—the standard, garden-variety

360 and the 180/180. The standard 360 is accomplished by starting with a forward 180, spinning the car until it's almost facing the opposite direction (say, 160 degrees), and then turning the wheel to continue the spin until the car is facing the same way it was before you started the whole grand maneuver, which probably wasn't done on purpose from the beginning. The 180/180 starts the same way, but when the car gets to the 180 position, it stops and spins another 180 in the opposite direction.

Here's the difference: Say you've started the car spinning right, or it's started itself spinning right; you've brought the steering wheel back to straight, and, as the car continues rotating, just before you get to 180, you turn the wheel in the opposite direction of the spin. And you hold it there. The car will continue spinning in the same direction, until it gets to a full 360 degrees, and then it will catch. For the 180/180, you turn the steering wheel in the same direction the car is spinning. It will stop at 180 and spin another 180 in the opposite direction. In other words, it is not a complete loop with the rear end always going in the same direction. On the first part it spins one way, and on the second part it spins the other.

Other than for a change of spinning scenery, the 180/180 would be used if you could see you were running out of room in the direction of your first 180 spin. But there is seldom time or space for a complete spin at all, let alone enough for you to make a decision as to which direction you want the car to spin next. But it is fun to practice. Just be careful in instituting either form of the 360, on or off the track. It is always better form to *prevent* a spin.

An important factor emerges in a spin, particularly a 180: When you're going backwards, everything obviously works in reverse, including the caster, so the wheels are no longer going to try to straighten themselves out. In fact, they are going to try to turn to lock, so you must get a good grip on the wheel or it will be jerked from your hands, sending you off to God knows where. The other major factor to think about is the braking system. We have already determined that most cars have approximately 80 percent of their braking force on the front. Well, these front brakes are now on the rear, with the weight moving in the other direction, forward. They are going to work like gang busters, so you will have to be very careful when applying pressure to them or they will lock up very quickly. It is perhaps the only place where you might want to *modulate* the brakes, that is, pump them gently as you would on ice. Take a deep breath and e-e-e-ase on the brakes.

If you watch a veteran race driver spin in a turn (see, it happens to them, too) and there's an outside wall in that turn, you'll immediately see the tires light up (start smoking). Since most cars spin to the outside of a turn, and he knows the wall is there, he has probably gotten on the gas in an attempt to keep the car spinning into the infield. That takes a lot of practice *and* experience. You won't want to get into that for a while.

But, if it happens that you're spinning toward an outside wall, and it comes to mind, get on the gas. You've got nothing to lose. This maneuver will spin you to the infield maybe 90 percent of the time. It's just not the kind of thing one *practices.*

If there's a wall on the inside of the turn where you're spinning, get *off* the gas immediately and let the car spin to the outside of the track. There are variables, of course, but these maneuvers work most of the time.

The key element in skid control is *timing.*

All maneuvers work best on dry pavement and worst on ice, because the more adhesion you have, the better the corrective measures will work. But the oiled skid pad is a wonderful simulator. You will be amazed at how well and how consistently it works. The car will do what you want it to, *if* you do the right thing. At the right time.

Turning Practice

A lot of the driving techniques seem very basic, while others appear complex beyond belief. You will be surprised in practice to see that the basic maneuvers are the important ones, and the complex ones are not all that difficult. You will have to *make* yourself do a lot of them, because they don't seem to come naturally. Like turning in later: You're not going to want to do it, but once you do and you feel it, you'll be surprised; you will just squirt right out of the turn.

Let's assume that you've been able to get the use of a parking lot at a shopping center or an industrial park or even a race course of some kind where you can practice your turns on weekends. Practice a lot before you even think of applying for an SCCA or an IMSA license. If it has become a club project, so much the better.

Here's how a practice course should be laid out, and how you should use it:

Place one cone at the left side to mark the turndown point, one on the inside of the turn to indicate the apex, and another at the exit point on the left side of the track. These should be precise points that you've first diagrammed on paper, showing where to turn in, exactly where the apex is, and where you should be at the exit. Place the cones and try it. If necessary, move them until everything is perfect for your proper late apex and arc.

Leave the car in second gear all the way around for the first few laps, because you will need to concentrate first on your line. Later you can work in the other elements and shift to your heart's content. But, while you are in second gear, pay particular attention to the engine revs. Stay well below the red line, and keep a close watch on the water temperature and oil gauge. If either of them climbs past the normal operating range, find out why.

Drive to the first cone at about 30 or 35 miles per hour, arriving with your hands in the crossover position; as you get right next to it, start feeding in the steering and begin the arc, which gets tighter and tighter to the apex —the second cone. Get tight, right next to the apex, and hold it there until the nose of your car is pointed in the direction of the exit cone. Begin to open up on the steering, and let the car go wide, coming out to the edge of the track at the exit cone.

You want to be 2 inches from all the cones, not 2 feet. If there's a wall or a building going in or coming out, perhaps you can drive to within a foot for the first few laps or until you get the hang of it, allowing for experience to get you closer. But eventually you must get in close because—and I can't stress this enough—these are precise points. If you are off by a foot going in, you will be off by several feet coming out.

You are now ready to add a few more cones. There should be three cones placed in a straight line before the turndown cone. The first should be at the point where you initiate the braking procedure—where you begin to squeeze on the brakes. A few yards from the first one, the second cone indicates where brake pressure is increased to hard braking—in a straight line. The next cone marks the spot where you start heel-and-toe downshifting, again a few yards down the course, toward the turndown point.

These new cones add importance to what was simply the turndown point, because it now represents *four* things: the point where downshifting is completed, the point where hard braking in a straight line is completed, the beginning of trail braking, and the point where you begin to turn in for the apex. This is all very important because every lap should be a carbon copy of the lap before. If you are having trouble with any part of the run, practice that particular technique until you are not only perfect, but perfectly consistent. Braking, for instance, should give a passenger—providing you have found one who will ride with you—the feeling that he doesn't know where it has started and where it has stopped—unless he is watching the driver's feet. It can't be stressed enough: All controls are like rheostats, and not like On/Off switches.

As for actual placement of the cones, some may change with speed, but most won't. Obviously, the turndown point, apex, and exit cones stay right where they are. There is only one proper late apex, so there is only one proper line to it and one away from it. These are fixed points, regardless of speed.

You may be starting at a slower speed and working up gradually to what you consider a competitive speed, so you may want to move the cones out, away from the turn a car length or two to give yourself a little more time initially. They should be placed so that you can comfortably complete the necessary operations before you get to the turndown point. You certainly don't want to reach that point in the wrong gear, with tires smoking and your hands in an awkward position on the steering wheel. Practice until you

A Bondurant Formula Ford in action.

are smooth, and then move the cones closer to the corner. Just make sure that you have left yourself enough room to complete everything smoothly. It may be a matter of experimentation.

You can place another cone on the outside of the track, at the point where you have stopped turning in, as a *guide* to keep you turning in the proper arc. The car is pointed directly at the apex at this spot, and the trailbraking is complete. You have started to roll on the throttle gradually, so that, as the steering begins to open up when you pass the apex, you are back hard on the throttle. And on your fast and merry way, confident in the knowledge that you have done it all very well.

It is important enough to go over again, step by step: As you approach the first cone, come off the gas and squeeze gently on the brakes, coming down harder in the next two or three car lengths as you reach the second cone. Don't jump on them and pitch the weight forward. By the time you reach the third cone, the car should be slowing down, so that's the time to begin your heel-and-toe downshift. Hard braking in a straight line and downshifting should be completed by the time you reach the all-important fourth cone, or turndown point. With your hands in the crossover position on the steering wheel, start feeding in the steering to begin the arc, which eventually will point the car in the direction of the apex. Continue trailbraking, keeping weight on the inside front wheel, as the car turns in more and more. Gently ease off the brakes and roll on the throttle as the nose of the car points in the direction of the apex. As you pass within 2 inches of the apex, you should be at full throttle, with the steering opening up. The car will accelerate smoothly to the exit point on the outside of the track.

The only thing that will change in this technique between 40 mph and

140 mph is the distance of the straight-line braking; but, regardless of speed, it has to be done by the time you reach the turndown point because, quite simply, that's where you finish going straight. Most people—even instructors—make it sound far too complex. After all, you are dealing with very basic principles; approach them that way.

Emergency Avoidance Techniques

The Bondurant School, like many others, uses an accident simulator to stress a highly important point: In almost every emergency situation, it is better to steer around an object in your path than to use your brakes. The school uses simulated traffic lanes with remote-controlled stop lights; you can simulate the simulator and, in so doing, prove it to yourself. But first, let's look at the principles involved:

We'll say a propane truck has stopped directly in your path, about 75 feet in front of you—you can make it a spinning race car if you wish, but there's just something so impressive about a propane truck. The first reaction is to back off the gas, which is a good one, but one which transfers the weight to the front. You know that in understeer conditions—where there is a lot of weight forward—you are going to slide right into the truck if you use the brakes heavily and lock up the front wheels. By the same token, if you lock up the rear wheels, the car will spin and you will hit the truck with the side or the back of your car; neither is a particularly attractive solution to the immediate problem.

In addition to backing off the gas, here's what you should do:

As the weight transfers to the front of the car and onto the front tire patches, the steering is in a condition to work well. So the solution is simple. Swerve to another lane. But you're not through yet. When the car is headed properly, bring the steering back to straight ahead. The car will have a tendency to oversteer because you have made the back end light and it can't do its job, which is to follow the front end, so you must immediately get some weight back there. So—you guessed it—get back on the gas. That will transfer some of the weight back, to tell the rear wheels to do what they were designed to do: follow.

It works anywhere.

The throttle is the key during this evasive action. It is directly related to where you want the weight; it's off the gas, giving the weight to the steering wheels to roll the front end over there, and back on as soon as it's headed properly, to get the weight to the rear wheels to make it follow. Off when you put the steering in, back on when you take it out.

If you have a car with a lot of horsepower, or if the pavement is wet, you must squeeze the power back on. Otherwise you will spin the rear tires, giving you wheel-spin oversteer, and you're still into the side of the propane truck. The way to do it all smoothly, is to practice it as recommended with the cornering technique, using pylons and an appropriate paved area.

To react quickly on the highway, race course, or solo course, it is imperative that you understand exactly what is happening to weight distribution in an emergency situation. After you have laid out a course, practice *both* the swerving and braking actions, and measure the results in terms of propane trucks wiped out.

Here is how you can lay out an accident simulator course:

You will need at least two or three people to assist you with the lane-change situations we are going to describe. You will also need to use a little ingenuity to indicate the open and closed lanes. Here is one suggestion (of course, if you can simply get three red lights and a remote control, so much the better):

Mark off three lanes with pylons, about 10 feet apart. In each of the lanes, place a plastic, gallon milk jug with a large red "X" painted on each side, and a string attached to the handle—it should be long enough to get the assistant well out of the way. Be sure to have plenty of extra plastic jugs. For obvious reasons. Mark off 75 feet forward of the three lane simulators and place two pylons 10 feet apart to indicate the entrance to the course. Your "course marshalls" (a fancy title in lieu of pay) should hold the strings taut as you enter the "gate," and, at that instant, they should jerk away two of the jugs, as an indication of which lane is closed—the one with the plastic propane truck. They should, of course, have a prearranged schedule, so that all three aren't jerked away at the same time. Or none. The open lanes should vary and, as the driver gets more adept, only one jug should be removed, giving the driver but one choice. The jugs must be removed precisely as the car enters the gate.

Start practicing at 30 mph and gradually increase the speed in 2 mph increments, until you can satisfactorily negotiate the emergency lane changes at about 50 mph. No faster. Look toward the center lane and allow your peripheral vision to work for you. The instant you see the lane open up, get off the gas, crank in the proper amount of steering to get the car headed toward the open lane, and, when it turns, bring the steering wheel back to straight and squeeze the power back on. Do not anticipate the open lane, because nothing about high-performance driving should be guesswork.

When you get to the point where you are missing more propane trucks than you are hitting, you can add the next element—braking. Braking will obviously require a three-lane red condition, so your helpers should—every third or fourth time—leave all three jugs in place to indicate that a braking maneuver is required. You must stop short of the jugs. If possible.

You know that the most efficient braking input is in a straight line, and should be as hard as possible without locking up the wheels. If you feel it in the wheel, it's front-wheel lock-up; if you feel it in the seat, it's rear-wheel lock-up. Or you may just smell essence of Goodyear. But, whatever the situation, back off the brake pedal enough to get the wheels rolling again. And don't turn the steering wheel, or the car will slide sideways.

You will quickly learn two things. Thing One: You have to constantly change brake pressure. Thing Two: You almost never stop in time. With practice, you can stop within a foot or two *past* the plastic jugs, but that just wouldn't help much if it were a truck or a wall. But keep practicing until the stopping distance gets shorter and shorter. It will help you in other emergency situations where stopping in time *is* possible.

Your score of swerving to avoid an accident as opposed to stopping will astound you, probably 20 to 1 in favor of swerving.

To summarize: Since you have added the braking dimension, you will need first to get off the gas and then analyze whether or not you need a brake input. If you do, squeeze on the brakes in a straight line and get the car stopped as quickly as possible, without leaving a trail of rubber behind you. If you have the opportunity to steer away, stay completely off the brakes and use the steering and the accelerator. You'll find that you have far more success with steering than with stopping.

Practice on highway or track. For one thing, deciding when to brake is the hardest judgment you'll ever have to make. Just ask someone if he can stop his car in a 75-foot distance from 40 mph. "No sweat," he'll say. Have him try it. The problem is that if you estimate the distance in which you think you can get stopped, you're probably going to be wrong. But if you estimate the same distance and say you are going to steer out of trouble, you're probably going to be right.

Look for a space to steer toward—an opportunity to swerve away—drive off across somebody's lawn, down through the infield, anywhere you won't hit anything or anybody, then come back onto the pavement just past the next-door neighbor's lawn on the next turn. But make very sure of where you are going; there's little point in swerving to miss a spinning car or a truck, only to plow into a pole. Or a pedestrian.

Keep two things in mind: If the area is clear, anything is preferable to tagging somebody in the truck or side, and a car simply does not stop as well as it maneuvers or avoids. Cars with anti-dive (nose down in hard braking) characteristics, like Porsches, come closer to it, but it is entirely possible, and highly likely, that you will overcome that anti-dive characteristic as well by pouncing on the brakes and overloading them.

5

Competing on the Track

The first competitor you have to beat is yourself. You must break any bad habits and form good ones, and then perfect them until they are instinctive. Along the way, you will have mastered your car and, finally, the track. Only then should you even think about getting on the track with anybody else.

When you do get into competition, it won't take you long to find out who is doing well out there. But don't be intimidated into doing something wrong. It is you who are responsible for protecting the line through a corner that you have set up—hopefully perfectly. Don't worry about the other guy's line, that's entirely up to him to protect. It is interesting to note that two drivers fighting each other usually go slower than they would separately, simply because they are trying to keep each other from passing, doing protective things, and not using the road efficiently.

You must learn to *drive* the track first, then learn to *race* it later. You will find that if you learn it all perfectly, you can outdrive 90 percent of the guys who have been out there awhile. That leaves only 10 percent to worry about. But if you don't take the time to learn the track, you'll have 100 percent of them in your way.

Races, incidentally, must be no shorter than thirty minutes duration, although they are usually set up by number of laps. No more than twenty-five cars per mile of race course may be started, so this means that if it is a 3-mile course, they can start as many as seventy-five cars. Seldom, however, are there even close to this many cars starting a race.

Playboy's Guide to . . . Sports Car Driving

As for the courses, they vary as greatly as the cars themselves. Some are twisting, tight, and flat, while others are uphill, downhill ones with long, fast straightaways. Practice and thorough knowledge of each course is obviously vital to good, safe, fast laps.

Here are some important things to look for once you get out on the track with other cars drivers who are trying to do the very same thing you have in mind—win:

All turns are important, but the *most* important ones are usually those leading onto a straightaway. And the fast turns. You can screw up a hairpin and it won't mean too much because it's so short, but if you screw up a fast turn, you've scrubbed off a lot of speed, and it's going to take time to build it back up. After all, when you're covering ground at a higher rate of speed, you want to maintain that speed as long as possible. Even a hairpin can be fairly quick if it is an increasing radius. In fact, to a great degree, the type of radius determines how fast any turn can be taken.

One way you can determine how well you have taken a turn is to look at the tach as you come out. If you're doing at least 4,500 rpm, you have probably taken it pretty well. But don't get overconfident and spin a tire coming out, just to get the revs up in a hurry, because a spinning tire means lost traction, which, in turn, means lost time.

If the wheel spins coming out of a turn, back off the gas and straighten out the wheel slightly. It is probably spinning because the turn is too sharp, and the weight has shifted off that particular tire.

Keep in mind what can happen on the race course. Extensive damage, such as that to the car above, has changed many people's minds about competition, so you must ask yourself if your bank account can stand—God forbid—such an accident.

Competing on the Track

When you are going much faster, you will find that nearly everything tends to happen late: You brake too late, you turn too late, you do everything too late. That's because you are constantly being surprised. It is all coming too soon. So you have to learn to think way ahead. Look far down the track, not immediately in front of the car—it's too late to do anything about what's happening there anyway. This is exactly the reason you moved through all stages of handling and performance in small increments, slow to fast—so that you wouldn't someday find yourself through Turn Four, saying "Damn, that was great," only to find yourself already at Turn Five. Unprepared. If it ever happens, regain your composure, get the rhythm back, and then try to catch whomever it was you were racing. Chances are, he's already beaten you in that turn.

Above all else, don't get to the point where you scare yourself. The old adage "If you don't spin at least once on each lap, you're not trying hard enough" is sheer bullshit. You should be as relaxed as possible at all times. If you go over the crest of a hill with white knuckles, you will never be able to properly feel the brakes, and it is very important that you do trailbrake there, simply to keep the wheels up under the chassis.

Everything must be light and smooth. Even if it is a 140-mph turn, try to relax as much as possible. Granted, even the most grizzled veteran gets a little wide-eyed in a super-fast turn, but he doesn't let it play on his mind. He gets ready for it, negotiates it smoothly, and goes on to the next one.

If you become tense, wait until you get to a straightaway, where you can work up your shoulders or flex your fingers or anything to help relax your muscles; just keep a good grip on the wheel and pay attention to what is happening around you. But, for a second or two there, try to unwind.

Watch your mirror for cars about to overtake you. Pick several spots where you can take your eyes away from the track for a split second to see what is going on behind you. Have other spots where you can regularly check your instruments, particularly the tach, oil pressure, and water temperature gauges.

Things are going to be different with each lap. You can practice your line until it is perfect, but once you get to the corner, traffic might dictate another line. Things change, so be prepared for those changes because the likelihood of always having the proper line for a turn are extremely remote. You will probably have to slow down a little more if you are off line. And the adhesion factor might be different out there in the boonies—the marbles some racers call the off-line area.

A good race driver practices different lines through a corner, because it is important to know how the car will feel and how it will respond to the various paths through a given corner. It all refines your skill. The important thing is to *know* the proper line, and to use it every time it is available to you.

You should always proceed with caution on an unfamiliar track. Take a few laps at 60 percent until you can tell how the car will handle on that track on that day. Don't progress too quickly. Nearly any car will handle well at 70 or even 80 percent, but as you get near the limit, the little idiosyncrasies of the machine become more pronounced—the understeer, the oversteer, the fading brakes, whatever. You may think there is something dreadfully wrong with the car, but it is probably just the speed bringing out a particular characteristic. The same thing happens with race drivers. Almost anybody can drive well at 60 or 70 percent, but only the superior driver can do it consistently at 95 percent.

If there are slippery spots on the track, you must anticipate them. When you get to them, you should be completely ready to cope with the problem. This usually means slowing down and getting ready to correct for a possible slide. If the car starts to slide, you can catch it long before it gets out of hand. Most slides are unexpected, to say the least. The drivers aren't ready to correct for them; so if you know there is oil or gravel on the track, get ready. You will be a step ahead of the driver who goes in like Jack the Bear and spins off the track.

You should never feel that things are happening too quickly. If you feel that you are going too fast, something is wrong. It probably means that you *are* going too fast. For you, at that time.

You must get to the point where you can stay ahead of your car, and anticipate all of the things that are about to happen—from the car's idiosyncrasies to the fast turns to the things that happen in front of you very suddenly. Your mind must work at least as fast as the speed of your car.

It really doesn't matter what the speed is. As was stated before, the most important thing that changes with speed is the distance of straight-line braking. The point where braking trails off doesn't change; it has to be completed by the turndown point. If you've come down from high speed, after hard braking, you are going to have a lot of weight on the front end, and the natural tendency is to get off the brakes and crank in the steering. But that is going to take all the weight off the front, leaving the front tire patches light, and sending you right into an understeer situation. The most important thing you are trying to do at the turndown point is turn; so if you can keep the weight on the front, you can make the front end turn better. This sounds highly repetitive, but it underlines the importance of every aspect of high-performance technique, which is even more vital when you are on the track with other cars.

Trailbraking is a way of keeping the car balanced. You are keeping the inside front tire from getting light and losing traction and, by doing this, you are using the brakes as a *handling* device. That is why exhaustive practice is required before you get into competition. You must know well the feel of each handling technique, and what each does to the balance of the car; you also must know how the feel changes at higher speeds, so that you can quickly adjust your inputs. Obviously, if you applied the same amount of pressure to the brakes at 40 miles per hour as you did at 140, you would come to a complete stop on the track before you got to the turn. Which, in any form of competition, is undesirable. We won't even go into the consequences of the reverse.

Yours will not be the only car on the course with the precise line through the turn, so it becomes vital that you take advantage of every turn, every lap. You can't lose even a fraction of a second per lap and still remain highly competitive. Thus, it is imperative that the entrance and exit to each turn be perfect. If you are spinning a tire coming out of a turn, for example, that means there is not enough weight on it. You must back off and straighten out the car slightly; but next time around, don't go into the turn quite so fast. You won't lose the time coming out. It only stands to reason that if the corner is sharper, you are going to have to slow down more going into it. But most drivers don't. They go in at the same speed and try to make the sharper corner, then end up going wide. Particularly, if you are making an apex later than before, you have to make a tighter turn, which means turning in later. This part is simple. But, before any of this, you have to brake harder. You must be going slower at the turndown point. The later you make the apex, the tighter the beginning of the turn is going to be and, consequently, the more you will have to be slowed down.

It is impossible to give exact instructions because each track is different. You will have to apply the basic techniques and work it out for each track, each corner.

The cars differ, too. A production class car (one that was designed for the street and is either driven exactly as it was produced or in a slightly modified state) will not, as a rule, handle as well or be as responsive as a sports racing class machine, which is one that was made specifically for racing. The sports racer will have better brakes, handle better, and probably go a lot faster because of a better power-to-weight ratio. It will also get you in over your head quicker if you are a driver with limited experience. It makes the production class a more reasonable starting point. But there certainly are exceptions to every rule. That is one of the things that makes racing a fascinating sport.

Few will have a chance to drive a Formula Ford—or any formula car, for that matter—but something should be said about this most popular class car because, if you ever do get the chance, you should know that it is a whole 'nother ball game.

Formula Fords require a different driving approach from any of the other classes. For one thing, they weigh only 900 pounds and have more than two-thirds the horsepower of, say, a Datsun 280-Z. Most of the weight is centered between the wheels of the single-seat, open-wheel racer. The clutch is very quick, so it is easy to kill the engine as you come out of the pits the first few times. Limited foot room makes it even more difficult to get used to clutch and brake application.

The brakes are much heavier—four-wheel disc with no vacuum assist—so they work much better than anything you have ever been used to, with none of the spongy feeling of most automotive brakes. You push hard on the brakes of a Formula Ford and the car stops fast; but you can lock up the wheels easily, so you must practice the proper pressure at slower speeds before you get into turns at higher ones.

The throttle is extremely good with progressive geometry, which gives you an outstanding response when you push the loud button (racer talk for the accelerator). This, linked with incredible power-to-weight ratio, makes it a potent performer.

Steering is one of the major differences between a formula car and a sports car. Again using the 280-Z for comparison, the Formula Ford's steering is exactly twice as responsive—one-and-three-quarters turn, lock to lock, as compared to three-and-one-half turns on the Z. Combine this with the small steering wheel on the formula car, and you have a very different feel, one that you will want to be highly familiar with before you go fast. If you go blasting into a turn at high speed in a Formula Ford without first getting used to the steering, you may wind up deep in the corn patch.

The car has far more tire surface in relation to weight than a sports car, so, in addition to stopping quickly, it moves in either direction extremely fast and with a great deal of stability. You have to be very careful at all times because the outstanding stability gives you a great sense of security; but it all goes away very quickly if you get in over your head.

You can't jerk on the steering wheel even the slightest bit or the car will be all over the track; so you must be very careful not to move the wheel when shifting. The shift lever is only about four inches high and is mounted high up on the right side of the cockpit, which is an odd feeling in itself. It only requires about one inch of movement to go from one gear to another —that is one-half inch from first to neutral and one-half inch from there to second. Mind boggling. You can shift with your fingertips, but the gears are not synchromesh, so you must snap it into gear briskly, otherwise the grinding noises will make you sound very unprofessional. The ratios are very close, so acceleration up through the gears can be very erratic if you don't get it all down smoothly.

Because of the tight steering, it should never be necessary to move your hands from the 3 and 9 o'clock position. A hairpin turn requires only about one-quarter turn, so you can pretty much forget about the crossover position, which is just as well because you will have a lot of other things to get used to.

One of the most important things to remember is to stay out a little farther from the wall and other obstacles because the rear wheels are wider than the front ones and there is a definite tendency to put the left side of the car in the same position as you would a sports car or a sedan. This, unfortunately, will put the rear wheel into the wall. It is also harder to judge left-side distance because you are sitting in the middle of the car; but once you get used to it, you can very precisely put the car where you want it. For one thing, you have the tremendous advantage of being able to look right out there and see exactly where the tire is in relation to the apex.

Don't get overconfident because the formula car sticks so well. It will spin easily if you do the wrong things. You can have absolutely no lapses of concentration. The same is true with *any* formula class car; it's just that there are more Formula Fords around than any other types, so it is likely to be the one you drive, if you drive any at all. But if you have the opportunity, do so. It may well be the most fun you'll ever have sitting down.

As for actual racing strategies, perhaps it might be premature to get into them at this point. There are so many variables, such as speed of the car versus experience of the driver and the number of racers and type of track. Specific strategy can best be learned as the driver progresses. On-the-job-training.

Using Flags to Your Advantage

A thorough knowledge of the flags used on a race course is imperative, simply because they are the best means of communication you have on a course. You may have a two-way radio, but what your pit crew tells you probably is not official, so you still must depend on the flags. You have to know their meaning, and you have to respond as if by instinct.

After learning exactly *what* the flags mean, you should know *where* they are displayed around the track; not all can be found in the same place. You can find out during practice where the flag stations are, so you will know where to look during the race.

Some flags are on stationary display and some are waved. A few can be displayed either way, but their meanings change depending on whether they appear waving or stationary. Learning what each one means is no easy task, but it is an important one because not only can the flags tell you what is going on, they can give you an advantage over the other guy if you respond immediately. And if you know some of the little tricks of the track. The plot thickens.

There are, of course, many rules of racing. Many rules. The flags will help you interpret them. By knowing exactly what is permitted, you can, well

. . . certainly not *cheat,* but you can definitely use the flags to your advantage. And stay just within the regulations.

Let's take a look first at how the SCCA explains the flags (IMSA, incidentally, uses the same system):

Directive flags inform the drivers of certain course conditions or of certain orders from the chief steward, and they require a certain response from the driver. These consist of the stationary and waving yellow, red, black, and black/orange (mechanical) flags.

Informative flags warn drivers of potentially dangerous course conditions or situations of which they should be aware but which do not require a response from the drivers. These include the striped yellow and red flag, the white flag, and the blue flag with a yellow stripe.

The stationary yellow flag tells the drivers that there is a car, emergency vehicle, or corner worker in a target area. This means that although there is no obstruction of the line, there is an obstruction close to it. Drivers are required to have their cars under control and may not pass another car from the moment they come to the yellow flag until they pass the accident area.

The waving yellow flag warns drivers that the line is either partially or completely blocked and that they must leave the line or perhaps the track surface to avoid the accident. Drivers may not pass from the moment they are opposite the flag until they cross the accident scene.

The striped yellow and red flag is called the oil, slick, or slippery condition flag. It informs drivers that oil, gas, water, gravel, sand, hay, mud, rocks, or other slippery substances—or hoods, engines, or small parts—have been spread on the track surface. It requires no reaction from the driver. Under racing conditions, the oil flag is displayed until there is an improvement in the course condition.

The white flag indicates that an emergency vehicle or a slow-moving race car is on the course. It requires no reaction from the drivers. It is displayed in the corner where the vehicle is and at one corner preceding, always held stationary.

The blue flag with a yellow stripe is displayed stationary and indicates a faster car is overtaking a driver, and that the driver should check the situation behind him, using his mirrors. This flag requires no action by the driver but is very important during qualifying, multi-class practices and during races when leaders begin to lap slower cars.

The red flag tells drivers that they must stop their cars as quickly as possible, clear of the racing surface, and wait for orders from the chief steward through corner personnel before proceeding. It requires immediate and complete obedience. Many regions display this flag only at the start/finish line.

The black flag indicates to the particular driver to whom it is displayed that he must proceed to the pits and must stop and confer with the chief steward or the assistant chief steward. The mechanical black flag or black flag with orange circle indicates to the particular driver to whom it is displayed that there is something mechanically wrong with his car. The driver must reduce speed considerably and proceed to the pits for repairs. Both of these flags require specific responses from the driver. A furled black flag warns a driver of a driving infraction which if repeated will result in an *un*furled black flag. Big brother is watching.

A green flag means the race is started and will continue at speed as long as it is displayed, and a checkered flag is just as obvious—the race is completed.

A clear course is indicated by the absence of other flags, although at some courses the green flag is displayed continuously at the start/finish line.

That is the *official* word on flags. Any variation from these rules places you in danger of being penalized. It could cost you far more than the slight advantage that "stretching" the rules might gain you. It is one of the basic rules of racing. However, let us take a look at some of the things some racers do—little tricks of the trade, if you will. They certainly aren't condoned by any of us, but, well . . . if nothing else, you should know what the *other* guy is doing. And some of these tips are perfectly legal and might give you a slight advantage.

On a green flag rolling start, you should try to get enough momentum so that as the flag drops, you turn the wheel and pass three rows of cars. That is what everyone strives for, and few achieve. Almost anything else on a start is illegal. But if you are starting in, say, 60th position, you can get by with a lot more, simply because the starter is busy watching the front of the field. Most racers can quickly figure out the situation by watching how the starter works in previous races or classes.

There are few standing starts any more because of the fender-benders that result from them, so when the green flag drops in a race, everybody starts, regardless of position. The cars way back are started long before they get to the starting line, so it becomes particularly important to them to be doing as well as possible as soon as possible. They must move up quickly.

A passing flag does not mean that you have to give up your line through a turn. In fact, you should *not* give up the line at all. And, unless you get the blue flag with the yellow stripe, there is no reason at all to let a driver by. Officially. But it is good sportsmanship, so long as it does not affect a battle you may be having with another car. When practicable, let the other car pass. Point to whichever side you want him to use to overtake you; you may even want to slow down a little to make it easier for him, but only if it does not affect your efforts in your class. Above all, don't give up your line; for one thing, it might put you in the precarious position of getting out of line and losing control, which often goes with it. It is, after all, his problem to get past, not yours.

The passing flag can be welcome at times, like, say, at Daytona, where one car can be doing 120 miles per hour and the other 200. It is nice to be warned that a 935 is barreling down on you. On the other hand, it is comforting to you as a 935 driver to know that the other guy is aware that you are coming through.

If a car is gaining a few seconds on you with every lap but still is not ready to pass, and you get the flag, ignore it completely. As for actual blocking, that is illegal at all times. On the last lap, however, it is sort of legal because you have one lap to move over, and by then the race will be over. It is stretching the point a little.

There is no question, however, that if you block—even if you don't get caught—the guy you have blocked will rightfully be irritated, and, if he's somebody like George Follmer, he may drive over you. So it is important to know who it is you are holding back. But if you are second and the other guy is third, well, who can tell you what is the best thing to do? There is a fine line between sportsmanship and finishing second.

Race drivers are big on "rules of thumb," so here is a popular one: It is best not to drive by the mirror. How do you avoid that? Simple, according to many: Drive the fastest car, and then look through the windshield. That, unfortunately, is not always possible, so you must use judgment and caution at all times, and drive as fast as is comfortable and legal.

Caution (yellow) flags are another matter of judgment. Just how much you slow down is usually up to you, but you should always be *ready* to slow down because any one of the three yellow-flag situations indicates that all is not well on the race course. In short, stay alert but keep your speed up as long as you possibly can. Novice drivers should follow the flags a lot more closely than experienced drivers, simply because they are under stricter scrutiny by race observers around the track. This means that the novice can't get by with as much, so he has to keep a lower profile.

One way to look as if you are slowing down under caution is to shift to a gear higher than you would normally use during race conditions. Lower revs means lower speed to an outside observer, but you won't have as good an exit coming out of the corners, so be prepared to get on the gas a little harder. On waving yellow, if you drive *smoothly* through the corner and put your hand up, the corner man probably will assume you have slowed down. If you are smooth and your tires aren't screaming like mad, your speed never seems as great to others.

Arrange your line to get maximum exit speed around a car that has spun out. If there are no other cars around, you can even use it as an apex. But you must always be as inconspicuous as possible.

If you see the yellow way ahead, you can usually get by a car or two before you get to it—more if they have slowed down early—but if you start to put a wheel under somebody just as you come to the flag, that's stretching it too far. The opening statement on yellow flags bears repeating: Caution (yellow) flags are a matter of judgment.

If yellow flags are displayed all the way around the course, it probably means that you are going to get a red flag next time around, so flags give you a general awareness of exactly what is going on out there. Pay strict attention, even if you feel you are aware of the situation, because the mere fact that a particular flag is out doesn't necessarily mean that the other guy has noticed or will react to it. When people get in cars and their adrenaline starts flowing, strange things can happen. It is a time when common sense —and maybe even the ultimate concession, slowing down—can make a difference.

At Riverside a few years ago, a car spun and the driver used all the knowledge anybody could have used. It was obvious that he was not going to be able to stop the slide, so he let it spin 180 degrees, caught it, got it going straight backwards until it was clear there wasn't anybody around, and then he spun it the rest of the 360. The car spun off the track without touching anybody or anything. It was a marvelous example of regaining control. But, as they say in racing, he ran out of brains. As the yellow flag went out, the driver pulled back onto the track without looking. He pulled right into the path of an oncoming car that hadn't slowed down for the yellow, and he got T-boned at 150 miles per hour. He had done everything right, up to the point of reentering the track. So, you see, flags don't communicate common sense.

The black flag is one that most drivers ignore as long as they possibly can. You may be dropping a wheel off the track in Turn Four every time you go through, causing a dangerous situation because of all the gravel you are spreading on the track, or you may simply be leaving a trail of smoke. Whatever the case, if you see the black flag and are in a pack of cars, you may be able to ignore it for a lap or two. Until they put out the black flag with your car number on it. You have no choice at that point, friend. You must come in the next time around. You have pushed it as far as they are going to allow you to push it.

If you are merely trying too hard to improve your position under yellow (you don't always get away with it) or almost any time you are trying to gain a few seconds questionably, they will black-flag you if they notice it; the little you gain usually won't be worth it, particularly if it costs you a minute or two as the guy slowly walks up to your car, crosses his arms, and starts the conversation with, "Are you the one who . . ." By the time you promise him you will never, ever, do it again, you may have lost a whole lap.

But if there is only one lap to go, you might want to totally ignore the black flag.

The mechanical black flag indicates that you have some sort of mechanical problem. Simple. If you know what it is, and you are sure it won't hurt anything, ignore it as long as you can. But if the guy holds up the black flag with the orange ball and he has a horrified look on his face, it may be something you don't know about, so *slow down* and come into the pits.

In a white-flag situation, just pay attention, but don't use the emergency vehicle as an apex. There could be a touchy situation there. And, if you should find yourself in an oval track race, the white flag there usually means one lap to go, so you should drive like hell.

When you slow down for any flag—or any situation—you should always hold up your hand. If you are the one who is crippled, run to the outside or, better yet, completely off the line where the fast groove is; it is not only courteous, but smart. It might keep you from being hit in the rear.

If you are coming up on a crippled car, be extra cautious, because, even though he might be off the line, he may be getting ready to *cross* and enter the pits. Watch for his hand signal.

The oil flag is displayed differently at different tracks. Some wait until a car spins, while others display it the minute they see smoke coming from a car. Whenever you see it the first time, brake a little sooner, hold up your hand, and look for the oil. See what it takes to drive around it, and watch for other cars. Go as fast as you *safely* can. When the track appears dry, and you want to try it, put the inside wheels in and see if it is still slippery, but be prepared for the car to let go so you can correct for any slide before it happens. If the track feels slippery, drive a few more laps and try the same thing again. Make sure it is completely dry before you get back in the line at speed; but get back as soon as you possibly can.

After the checkered flag, you are supposed to back off, but it's not all that wise to back off too much. You may have drivers that are still keyed up or maybe angry because they lost, or perhaps they want to take one more fast lap before they hand it up, so you can get rear-ended if you slow down too suddenly. You should be even more careful about the other guy now than during the race. It is an extremely erratic time.

From green to checker, learn the flags and use them to your advantage. Just don't push your luck with rules or safety.

On Buying Equipment

When you buy an article of racing clothing or equipment, *don't try to get a deal.* You can't put a price tag on your own safety, and if you get burned because you bought a cheap driving suit or you weren't wearing Nomex (flame resistant) underwear, there is no replacement. This is perhaps Cold, Cruel Fact of Racing Life Rule Number One. It can happen to anybody, veteran or novice.

Every article of equipment, from the helmet to the shoes, should be (1) approved, (2) say so right on it, and (3) be the best you can buy. Otherwise, don't go racing.

The race car itself does not always have the ultimate in protection—there are simply too many things that can happen—so the driver must have it. Buy a Phase Three driving suit (a type, not a brand). It is a four-layer Nomex suit, but it breathes. And wear Nomex underwear. The rules don't require this, but it is an absolute necessity. If there is no insulation, you may get burned from the heat, and the underwear will insulate. Some suits will protect you from the flames but not the heat and, if you are lying in a hospital bed, trying to determine what went wrong with the trick suit, it will be little consolation to find out then. The important thing is not to get burned at all.

It is even better, in fact, to wear a five-layer suit and two layers of underwear. Don't rationalize how much cooler you are going to be with fewer layers of Nomex, because it isn't true in the first place. For one thing, the multi-layer suit breathes and, as you sweat into it and the underwear, it becomes wet and the air flowing through will actually cool you. You will be much cooler with seven layers that breathe than with one that doesn't.

You can tell the guy who has never been in a fire. He is the one running around the pits in a super-thin driving suit.

The rules don't call for a Nomex hood unless you have either long hair or a beard, but don't pay any attention to that either. A hood only costs about $10, and it protects the one area of your body that is always visible. You can cover up most of the other scars, but not the ones on your face.

If any of your clothing ever comes apart, make sure it is sewed up with Nomex thread, because if you get in a fire and the suit opens up, there is no protection at all. For exactly the same reason, a one-piece suit is better than a two-piece. It doesn't open up when you wrench yourself out of the car in some weird position. At a time like that, you don't want the top part of your suit to ride up and expose your midsection. Straps on your shoulders are particularly important if you are driving a formula car, because you can be pulled out by them. They are helpful in any car but should be mandatory in formula cars; it is often the only way anybody can get to you because there certainly isn't room to get under your arms. Straps that run from chest to back are better than the epaulet type that run from collar to shoulder seam, but either will work if they are securely fastened to the suit.

Don't ever work on your race car in your driving suit. If you get grease or gasoline on the suit, it will burn. But if you do soil it, Nomex can be washed in a washing machine; this is better than dry cleaning, which tends to destroy the thread and elastic. Dry Nomex material normally.

The gloves need to be at least five layers thick, or the thickest you can get and still maintain complete and accurate control of all the controls in the car—from steering wheel to shift lever. Gloves are highly important because if you ever get in a fire, your hands are the first things you will use to get out, and you'll probably have to put them right in the fire to boost yourself out. The proper gloves will give you about one-and-a-half minutes' protection in full flame.

An economic tip: Try to avoid buying equipment at the race track because the exact same items available elsewhere will probably be more expensive there. Also, the selection usually isn't great, so you might not be able to find the size or type you want. Find yourself a reliable outlet away from the track and take as much time outfitting yourself as you would your car. Make sure everything fits, and that it is exactly what you want in terms of style, protection, and quality.

As for shoes, buy leather boots or ones made of approved fiber. Use Nomex strings and Nomex socks, and don't even think about wearing tennies; the rubber will burn. Enough said.

It is not necessary to wear anything under your Nomex socks or underwear, unless you have a tendency to develop a rash from the material, which many people do; in that case, wear a thin pair of socks, a T-shirt, or whatever is necessary to keep the Nomex away from your skin.

Drivers usually wear their suits around the pits because they are bothersome to put on and take off—and, hopefully, they are cooler—but don't wear your fiber driving shoes when you are not driving, simply because they wear out quickly and, at $50 or so a pair, you want to get as much wear as possible.

Most people buy a good helmet because it is the one most noticeable part of their outfit and they want others to know they have the best. In this case, vanity pays off. You definitely want your head protected. Buy a good helmet, such as a Bell, and make sure it has the Snell Foundation stamp of approval on it. The Snell label is required at the race track but not for motorcycles, so it usually isn't a good idea to buy an auto racing helmet at a cycle shop.

If you get your helmet banged, with or without your head in it, or if the padding becomes compressed after much wear, send it back to the manufacturer, who will usually repair it for a small fee. If you crack it from, say, hitting your head against the roll bar, most good companies will fix it for nothing because they feel sorry for the guy who was inside it.

The face shield should be made of Lexan, and you should always wear one in a formula car because it is easy to take a rock in the face. The shields do fog up in the rain, so if you're wearing one, you should drill tiny holes in the bottom of it to let the air in. It works. Some helmets and shields have air passages to prevent fogging, so this may be another consideration when you are shopping around for the proper protection for your head and face.

Some of the newer helmets with intricate face masks designed into them must be fitted very carefully. In fact, fit is very important in any helmet.

A helmet shouldn't make your eyes pop out or give you cauliflower ears, but it also shouldn't rattle around on your head. A snug but comfortable fit will give maximum protection, so obviously you shouldn't borrow somebody else's helmet. It surely won't fit properly, and you won't know anything about its condition—whether or not it has been damaged. Weight is the final consideration in a helmet. At high speed, your head gets pulled around a lot from the G forces in the turns, and a big, heavy helmet accentuates this, making your neck muscles tire sooner. It is possible to get a lightweight helmet of high quality. Heavy isn't always best. In fact, it almost never is in racing.

6

Solo Competition

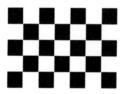

The SCCA Solo Events Program is divided into two basic categories of events: Solo I and Solo II. In broad terms, Solo I events are single-car speed competitions which require many of the safety measures used in racing. Consequently, they are not as popular because they exclude most of the weekend "fun" group. Solo I borders on professional racing. Solo II events are single-car, nonspeed competitions, which place a greater premium upon precision driving than all-out speed.

Because they are tailored to the average driver in his daily transportation automobile, Solo II events are far more numerous than Solo I's. Over 600 Solo II events under the SCCA banner in a single year contrast with perhaps two dozen Solo I events.

Solo II events—gymkhanas, autocrosses, slaloms, traloms, and field trials —are part of the weekend participant sports scene in almost every sizeable American city. They may be held on parking lots, open fields, and, in the winter, frozen lakes. Given enough room and several motorsport enthusiasts, a Solo II–type event will usually materialize with amazing rapidity.

No matter what they are called, these "track meets on wheels" are the most popular form of motorsport in this country. These closed-course, time-and-maneuver-ability events place an emphasis on the deftness of the drivers and the agility of the cars. Because they are inexpensive for the participant, they form the best driver education available.

Solo Competition

Hazard, and not *speed,* distinguishes a Solo II event from a Solo I. "It is," according to the SCCA's Solo II rules, "quite possible to set up a course on which speeds do not exceed 50 miles per hour, but which is much more hazardous than another course on which 80 miles per hour is attainable.

"If, for example, we take two identical 30-mile-per-hour turns, one bordered by a 50-foot dropoff or a solid row of trees, and the other bordered by 50 feet of smooth asphalt, the hazards involved are much different."

It is a rule of thumb that 45 miles per hour is the maximum safe turn speed for an inexperienced driver in an automobile with production suspension and street tires.

The challenge of the Solo II event is essentially "you against the clock." The human animal needs to gauge himself against his peers, however. The profusion of car models and types, with great differences in acceleration, braking, and maneuverability, make it essential that they be segregated into competitive groups.

The SCAA Solo II rules classify the full range of imported and domestic sports cars, sedans, and all-out racing cars. The organizers of local events are allowed enough leeway to add classes to suit their particular requirements.

The variety of classes offer many chances to take home a trophy for your Sunday sport in a Solo II event. This fits in perfectly with the basic "fun" premise of the program.

Solo II events are, simply stated, as complicated and the courses are as long as the area on which you are competing allows. Obviously a shopping center course will be shorter and possibly more demanding than one set up at an airport. But there is always a slalom segment with cones, and it would be extremely unusual if you got any practice runs at all. You generally get three timed passes through the course—one car at a time, of course—and that's it.

The rules are quite simple: The car that makes it through the course in the fastest time, hitting as few cones as possible, because that adds penalty points or time, wins. As in other forms of competition, there are various classes, so you won't have to run your Cadillac hearse against a Lotus Esprit.

Gymkhanas, autocrosses, slaloms, and field trials are merely different names for solo competition.

The Sunday afternoon Solo II event at the local shopping center attracts ordinary sports and sports-type cars used for daily transportation. Their owners inflate the tires to more than normal pressures, remove the hubcaps, empty the interior of loose items, buckle the seat belts, and have a go.

While the name of the Solo II game is fun, the events are a valuable stepping-stone for drivers who would someday move into racing. But most importantly they provide useful lessons for the driver who merely wants to become more proficient in his daily driving.

Tips from the Master

Whether you join an already established SCCA Solo II event or you want to set up your own, the advice of E. Paul Dickinson is invaluable. There is nobody more eminently qualified to give advice on Solo II competition than Dickinson, primarily because he is a five-time national champion, but mostly because he has never been defeated in national competition. Heavy qualifications.

"There's no room for a driving error in this sport because you're timing to one-hundredth of a second," says Dickinson. "You can, and often are, beaten by one one-hundredth of a second, so you have to be able to make quick decisions; you have to be able to think on your feet quite well.

"Solo is grass-roots racing, and you'll find it on all levels of competition —from supermarket parking lots to airports. In one event in Portage, Indiana, they shut down the city and race in the streets, and in Columbus, Ohio, they run at a one-mile speedway. They race anyplace they can get permission, and in anything, from a Sprite to a Corvette."

Dickinson's solo driving school is based in Huntington, West Virginia, but he moves it around from time to time, giving enthusiasts in other areas a chance to learn the sport. And learn they do. For $750 he totally immerses a student in a three-day course, eight hours a day, and evening chalk and film sessions.

"One can earn a doctorate degree in driving," says Dickinson. "Not just solo. You can find out what your weaknesses are and what your good points are. We simply try to strengthen the weak points and build on the good ones, making a competitive driver out of you. In racing you're battling with the guy in front of you, but in solo, you're racing the clock and you'll never beat it. So you have to become competitive with yourself.

"The basic techniques," says Dickinson, "are hand and eye coordination and proper placement of the hands on the steering wheel—three and nine o'clock. The latter may sound overly simple, but keep in mind that there

A Porsche 911 driver practices for solo competition.

are a *lot* of hand-over-hand turns. I mean, some guy may put a pylon at the end of a straightaway and say 'Okay, make a one-eighty here,' and at eighty-five or ninety, your hands had better be in the right position, ready to cross over and pick up the spoke of the wheel. Ready to make the right move in a hurry."

Dickinson is an efficiency expert in the area of driving. He begins with hand and eye coordination, then progresses to hand and eye and foot. He works with cones that exist and imaginary gates that don't—illusions and real road edges.

"Visual acuity," he says, "is paramount—how you use your eyes. I mean, you won't be allowed to practice the course before you run it, so you have to depend on efficient use of the eyes when you do. And before. You can walk the course, draw it, do anything you want short of driving it, and it is wise to know every square inch of it, analyzing each turn, each pylon.

"My personal philosophy is to bust the course on the first run. Many times the first run is the winning one. If you put in a good, strong run the first time out, it tends to demoralize the competition. A lot of drivers take it easy the first time out, sort of feeling their way through, but I like to have a fast initial run. For one thing, it gives me a good, strong base to fall back on. On later runs, you may knock down a pylon or make any sort of mistake, and if you have this good run to rely on, it may save the day."

Solo is the kind of sport that requires a lot of practice, particularly if you can't take classes in it. Get permission to use a shopping center parking lot after the stores have closed and set up your own solo course. Pylons are expensive, so you can use empty plastic gallon milk cartons or cheap plastic buckets.

The best course to set up is a serpentine of ten cones on a 50-foot center. You can learn 90 percent of what you need to know on that type of course. You can learn hand placement, hand to eye to foot coordination, apexing, turn speeds, the whole ball game. And, even when practicing, it is wise to diagram the serpentine to determine the proper apex before you run it. Then, after the practice is over, go back and annotate it. If you had trouble with a particular area, note it, along with the reason you think you had the problem. It will be useful later.

"As for eye coordination," Dickinson notes, "the problem most people have is in tunnel driving. If you put the cones a football field apart, I mean, each one way out there on the visual horizon, most people would tend to tunnel drive each one, so that just as they are passing by it, they would quit looking at it and look at the next one. Wrong. No matter how far apart the cones are, by the time you get to the first one, you should be looking way beyond the last one. You must work on developing your visual acuity to the point of being able to see not only that horizon, but everything between there and the nose of the car.

"It's more a matter of keeping the cones in perspective, being able to see all of them. What's immediately in front of you is history—you can't do anything about it—and what's way out there is history in the making.

"Solo is really no different from driving a car on a track or through a tight back road. In taking a hundred-and-eighty-degree turn, for example, you actually have to apex it. You don't just drive down there and turn left. You are dealing with a cone that can be knocked down.

"A vehicle rounding a corner has what is called 'rear-wheel cheat.' As this vehicle rounds a turn, just because the front wheels are steerable and the rear wheels are fixed, the rear end will 'cheat' on the front end. As you go around the corner, the rear end will cut a tighter arc than the front.

"So you must take a look at early, classic, and late apexes. If you take an early apex on the pylon in a one-eighty, the odds are close to a hundred percent that you'll knock it down because of rear-wheel cheat. If you take a classic apex (right in the middle of the turn), the odds are fifty-fifty. But if you take a late apex, the odds are zero percent of knocking down the cone. So, with knocked-over cones usually carrying a two-second penalty, you can't afford to knock any of them down. Even though the late apex might not be the fastest line, in this case it's the best because you can't afford the two seconds. In other words, if there's any question in your mind, *you should late-apex a turn.* It's a philosophy that's been around for many years."

Brakes and tires are obviously highly important to the solo car, so you must make sure that both are perfectly suited to car and course. The brake linings should be run in the same way they are for racing, because green linings will fade when heated and solo driving heats them. Make sure there is no moisture in the lines because it will boil and create steam, which means you'll probably lose most of your braking action. If the brakes get hot enough, a gaseous layer will form between the pad and the disc, so you may want to drill one-quarter-inch holes across the face of the rotors to allow this gas to escape. The holes will also help drain off water, which is desirable during rain because brakes can hydroplane just like tires.

As for tires, Phoenix 3011s are very popular with expert solo drivers, as are Goodyear Wingfoots and Eagles and Pirelli P6s and P7s. But there are

A Triumph in solo competition.

others that work well for each particular car. You should talk with someone who has a car similar to yours, and who seems to have things worked out well on the course before you spend $125 or so for each tire.

"As odd as it sounds, braking is a function of acceleration," says Dickinson. "Once the car is moving, you have wind forces that are constantly trying to slow you down; but when braking, you have things that work in your favor. A car accelerating from zero to sixty will take a certain distance; decelerating will take much less distance, so you stand to gain or lose more time with the brakes, depending upon whether you use them properly or improperly.

"The fastest and most efficient way to stop a car is by not locking up the brakes. For one thing, if you do, you melt the rubber and it forms little ball bearings of rubber that the tires slide along on. So you should brake at the 'impending skid' stage, which is just short of locking up the wheels—so close, in fact, that even the slightest additional pressure would lock them up. You must train your brain and your foot to know exactly where that point is."

Basic Law Number One, according to Dickinson: "If you enter a turn at or above maximum in any car with pneumatic tires, the vehicle will understeer, no matter where the engine is located or no matter who the driver is, so understeer *and* oversteer are tendencies that are as much driver-created as car-created.

"The ideal approach," he says, "is to develop a 'self-compensating' method of using oversteer and understeer. Create oversteer—by getting off the throttle—then understeer by getting back on. Repeat it if necessary. It's called stair-stepping, and it will scrub off enough speed to get you through in a sort of 'neutral' effect. It might not always be the fastest way through a turn, but it may be the *best*. If you can use a driving technique that will allow you to keep your speed up—to go very fast, but maybe not *as* fast as you could—and make few if any mistakes, you'll do well.

"The old adage, 'He who makes the least amount of mistakes in a day will win,' is more true in solo than in any other sport. If you're not a good technical driver with good technical skills, your finishing place will reflect it. But if you do drive into a turn a bit above maximum, you can salvage it by the self-compensating technique.

"If you find yourself five-tenths of a second slower than a competitor, you don't have to make all that up on one turn. Maybe you can correct a mistake exiting a turn, and, what with a long straightaway, if you clean up *one*-tenth on the exit, then you may have the five-tenths *plus* at the other end of the straight.

"Slow can be fast," he says. "The name of the game is smoothness, concentration, consistency, and accuracy. If you are smooth, you will have the concentration necessary to be consistently accurate. And that wins solo events."

7

The Rally

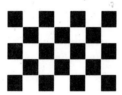

"Rallying is a fascinating, demanding, competitive game of navigational and driving skill," says SCCA publicity chief Mac DeMere. "It has been called a parlor game for adults, played outdoors on the open road, with cars. It has been described as a drive in the country to Grandmother's house— only you don't know where she lives and you don't know how to get there, but you have to arrive exactly on time. You might think of it as a kind of chess game in a vehicle."

There are various kinds of rallies. The most common type is the time-speed-distance rally (TSD), which has two basic characteristics: First, the contestants must follow the route instructions; and second, they must come as close as possible to the prescribed average speeds. The goal is to arrive at checkpoints along the way at precisely the correct time.

Route instructions might look like this:

1. Right at traffic light; begin average speed of 42.
2. Left on second paved road.
3. Right after Gulf Station
4. Left on Dry Fork Road
5. Right at stop sign [and so forth].

"An experienced rally driver can maintain a speed very close to the one that is specified, in this case, forty-two miles per hour, for several miles while the navigator calculates the precise amount of error. Through practice, rally skills can be developed," says DeMere.

"Rallying appeals to people of all ages and professions. If a person likes a drive in the country on a Sunday afternoon and likes to participate in competitive games of skill, then he or she will enjoy rallying.

"SCCA offers national championships in two kinds of rallying. Pro rallies include a number of high-speed special stages on challenging roads that have been closed to the public. Club rallies, on the other hand, are conducted on public roads and at speeds that are at or below the posted speed limits."

What distinguishes a rally from other types of SCCA events?

1. A rally is run on public roads.
2. Speeds are assigned, generally well below the posted limits.
3. Each rally course is unique.
4. The regulations for each event vary to some degree.
5. A contestant is competitive with little or no investment.

Club Rally Programs

The SCCA National Club Rally Championship is a highly successful series of national club rallies and divisional club rallies that are designed— and properly so—for the experienced rally enthusiast. Yet, at each of these events a fairly large number of inexperienced contestants enter and subsequently encounter the bitter experience of getting in over their heads.

These neophyte rallyists compete in the national championship events because most regions don't offer a series of less complicated events. And without a regional program to serve as the training ground, the new and potential members of SCCA find a local rally club in which to compete. They then lose interest in SCCA.

"Since a rally can be organized to be run any time and any place," DeMere points out, "the regional program can easily be incorporated into the social activities of the region, thereby getting all the members of the region involved.

"The type of rally program recommended places great emphasis upon 'fun' events while providing the groundwork through which the basic and necessary rudiments of 'club rallying' can be effectively taught and readily learned.

"Implementation of the ideas presented here will not be difficult and can be effected by the members who have little or no rally experience.

"An active rally program will be rewarding, since new people, ideas, and competition will pervade its activities.

"But most of all, the rally program should be fun—for organizers and contestants alike," DeMere concludes.

Rally Ideas That Work

Various clubs have conducted innovative rallies or rally themes. This list is not inclusive, but it is presented to inspire ideas which would be particularly effective:

- Rally to the club meeting or rally from the monthly meeting to a party.
- 7–11 rally. Trophy winners are those contestants who finish in seventh and eleventh place in each class.
- Rally competition for local radio/TV personalities as part of a series rally. Features free advertising and large entry.
- Rally to a resort area for the weekend.
- Rally to the races.
- Competition between the racing and solo enthusiasts.
- Charity events; all or part of the entry fee goes to charity.
- Veteran/rookie rally. Each vehicle has an experienced and an unexperienced contestant, selected by draw.
- Two clubs organize rallies to an intermediate location and have a joint meeting, picnic, or party.
- Rally to breakfast. Start at 3 or 4 A.M. Run in remote areas.

A rally schedule can include a mix of events. For example, a championship series of five or six events can be interspersed throughout the schedule, with contestants earning points toward year-end awards. The goal of the program should be to provide at least one event per month.

The championship-points events should be TSD rallies, in order to provide the training ground for the national and divisional club rallies that the contestant will enter.

In addition, a monthly meeting of all rallyists can include items of business, discussion of coming events, rally techniques, a movie, etc.

The Rally

How to Plan a Rally (As prescribed by the Sports Car Club of America)

You're likely to find that you've been carrying the germ of an idea for a rally with you for some time—that without conscious thought on your part, it has been taking shape. You have driven over a group of back roads, noticing the way they present a pattern of turns, dead ends, winding roads, and potential puzzles, and you think you can mesh these with secondary roads and a patch of highway to devise an intriguing, 60-mile rally route.

But your planning routine does not begin on the route itself; it starts in your living room or den, where you organize the general outlines of the event and the course. It begins with your finding answers to a number of questions:

1. Is this to be an afternoon or an evening event?
2. How many hours should it last?
3. What approximate speeds will you designate—and are they suitable to the roads, the safety demands of the route, the hour, and the normal flow of nonrally traffic in the area?
4. Can you expect a considerable number of workers, or must you plan an event requiring a minimum force of officials?
5. Will the rally be made up of several individual legs, or are you going to plot it as one overall run?
6. Need it begin and end at specific points, terminating for example at a favorite watering spot?

Pro rally driver John Buffum powers his TR-7 around a turn in a typical high-performance rally situation. In 1977, Buffum, with backing from British Leyland Motors Inc., won the Sports Car Club of America Pro Rally Championship.

7. What kind of checkpoints are you going to use: hidden, known, or unknown?
8. Will directions be given in terms of street names, mileage, time, description of landmarks, compass bearings, or a melange of these?
9. Will the rally have gimmicks?

One answer, of course, may affect several others. If your club is a small one, you'll be able to count on relatively few workers, and that fact alone may dictate a modest number of checkpoints. Or if the membership is made up for the most part of men and women new to the sport, you'll not want to discourage them with almost insuperable navigational problems. Choose a format that's fun, challenging, and compatible with the abilities of the membership.

When you have rough-hewn your rally by making these decisions, you'll next want to be sure that your new mental image of the event jibes with the route you've selected. Spread out several road maps of the area—as many different makes as possible. Work out the movement of the event, its start and finish points, intersections to be avoided, and its mileage. Our experience has been that the route invariably turns out to be somewhat longer than anticipated; in the advance work at home, then, we usually leave about a 10 percent margin for expansion.

Run the Route

Now at last you've reached the point where you can go out and run the route. This is not a job to be done alone; it calls for one person at the wheel and another to make meticulously detailed notes all along the way. The data you collect on this trip will be the basis of your rally-route instructions.

Take along a clipboard, an assortment of gas-station road maps, appropriate large-scale maps if you can secure them, and a legal pad. Legal pads have a vertical line running down their length, about one-and-a-quarter inches in from the left-hand edge of the paper. Mileages can be written to the left of this line, and other data to its right. After some 2 miles of driving, your log might look something like this:

> 00.00 START: Barney's garage. Turn right.
> 00.76 Right turn on Fox Meadow Road.
> 01.20 Straight (avoid road bearing right).
> 01.50 Stop sign. Cross highway.
> 01.72 Acute left. No name dirt road.
> 02.12 Right on blacktop.

For your own guidance and information, you've noted mileages in hundredths of miles, despite the fact that almost all odometers read only in tenths. Perhaps you'll never use this detailed data; yet today you're a top detective at a station-house line-up, noting every feature and every facet and every mannerism of possible significance. You're acting on the assumption that it's better to have too much knowledge than too little. Ideas generate ideas, and two days after you run this route, you may come up with a slight change in the rally format. You'll be saved the inconvenience of another advance run of the route to get information for the "slight change" if you make a step-by-step picture of the terrain your first time out.

Make it a point, too, to run the whole rally at once. And if that's not possible, at least run the individual legs as complete elements, using the same car so you're not changing odometers in midstream. Many an attractive rally has evolved into an atrocious fiasco because the planners of the event quit in midstream to go home for lunch and then picked up the route inexactly. No matter how stringent your precautions may be, it is almost impossible to pick up odometer mileages accurately.

Odometer Check

Whether or not you plan to include a check of each contestant's final odometer readings in the scoring of your event, you will insist that the rallyists adhere to prescribed average speeds; commonly, of course, they do this by reference to their odometers. You also know that odometers are inaccurate, and that their inaccuracy can be further compounded by such factors as varying tire pressures and the speeds at which the cars travel. Therefore, you'll want to set an arbitrary standard against which they can reckon odometer error for the run.

You should begin your rally by giving the contestants an opportunity to compare their odometer with your odometer. This is best accomplished by providing a 10–15-mile odometer calibration run involving numerous simple instructions, each accompanied by an official mileage. There should be a specific start point (odometer reading 0.00) and a specific end point for this odometer calibration run. Every effort should be made to ensure that the contestants do not lose the course.

A five-minute pause at the end of this odometer check is normal practice to allow the contestants time to perform calculations related to the differences between their odometer and yours.

The contestants will now be able to work out the difference between the official mileage and their mileage readings; they'll be able to correct their own odometer errors; and if you have not distorted the distance by inaccuracy or by the inexactness which comes from leaving a route and then "picking it up" again later, the rallyists have at least a chance to obtain a perfect score.

Checkpoint Locations

Your yellow pad is now as filled with detail and data as a corporate tax return. Yet one more set of notes is still to be made; you must observe and record suitable checkpoint locations. It isn't at all necessary to have each leg start and finish at control points, although it is customary. What is necessary is that you note any potential complicating factors when you mark off a location as an ideal checkpoint spot.

Is it on or near private property? Could activities there interrupt normal traffic? Is it a spot where passersby might cluster and stare, gabble and gawk? And if so, would this be a safety hazard? Or might they interfere with accurate checkpoint conduct? When you prepare your notes, make them broad enough to include alternate spots for checkpoints—perhaps a mile further down the road, or a mile back. List the possible problems.

The Committee

All you need now are contestants (readily available in all parts of the world) and a committee (people who would rather be contestants but have been talked out of it). You can't be at the start and at the finish and at all the checkpoints. You'll need others to help register, work checkpoints, and collect scorecards.

How many people make up a committee? Figure on at least two persons at each checkpoint, four at the start, and two more at the finish. Don't count yourself as one of these; you should not be tied down to any specific job, but should be left free to fill in wherever and whenever an extra hand is needed.

If there are three checkpoints in your rally, in other words, we recommend a staff of twelve assistants. This may be impractical.

Preparation

Duplication involves little expense, so you might as well go wild to the tune of a few dollars and produce twice as many sheets as you expect you'll need. For sure, you don't want to turn away an entry due to lack of instructions!

When your route instruction sheets are ready, call your committee together for a meeting. Explain how, and where, the rally is to be run; go over the whole question of timing in detail, explaining the system to be used. It's a sound idea to present a short course in reading a watch or clock at this meeting, with particular emphasis on such things as the "danger zone" between the 55- and 60-second points. Tell your committee whether the rally is to be timed "to the minute," "to the hundredth of a minute," or "to the second." Be sure they understand that no matter which it is, they must keep their records.

Go over the odd jobs to be done. Perhaps there's a checkpoint on private property—someone must see the owner and get his permission to use the spot. Or if there's a checkpoint on a public highway, someone must alert the police to the fact and get their approval. There are supplies to be amassed for the checkpoints, the starting line, and the finish line.

Perhaps most important of all details at this point is the question of timepieces. Many of the contestants in your rally will have spent small fortunes to equip themselves with accurate timepieces. They'll have stopwatches, timers, Rolex chronometers, and short-wave radio adapters. If you time them with an assortment of Mickey Mouse watches and drugstore alarm clocks, this will prove to be the most cordially hated rally of all time.

Most clubs have a supply of watches which are satisfactory for rally timing. At the start of the event, of course, all watches will be synchronized with whatever sort of accurate time you have chosen: network radio time tones, telephone time signals, or beeps from WWV or CHU.

Driving schools can give a driver a head start in racing and solo competition, but nothing short of time and experience will bring trophies to the rallyist.

The Sports Car Club of America has provided some sound advice from two experts on national rallying—Russ Brown, a former national champion navigator, and Jean Calvin, an ace driver.

Their rally tips are divided into three major segments: equipment, approach, and gamesmanship. It is not at all unusual for a rallyist to become proficient in the sport and never win or even come close to winning. And I doubt if there is one who falls into this category who can tell you why the winner's circle eludes him.

The winning rallyist is the one who prepares well in all three areas of rallying: good equipment, the proper approach, and sound gamesmanship.

Equipment

The most important piece of equipment, obviously, is the car itself. But, surprisingly, a lot of people run out and buy exotic timing and navigational devices without ever thinking of the car. Most rallies don't even have technical inspections, but that certainly doesn't mean you shouldn't have your own. Check the lights, tires, windshield wipers and washers, ignition system, brakes (lines and fluid), and exhaust system. And thoroughly clean all the glass.

A right side mirror for the navigator is helpful. For one thing, it enables him to keep track of any car that might be trying to pace you.

A lot of rallyists remove the hub caps, despite the effect this has on the aesthetic value of the machine. But removing the hub caps can save you a little time if you have to fix a flat en route. It may sound odd, but in a sport where the outcome is often decided in tenths or hundredths of a second, everything counts. It's a whole lot like a NASCAR pit stop. So you should practice tire changing in your driveway—with your navigator. Each of you should have a task, just like a regular pit crew. And make sure you take along on the rally everything you'll need to change a tire. Put your tools in an accessible place. You certainly don't want to have to take out the picnic basket and the thermos and all the jackets and equipment just to get the jack.

Even if a rally is to be a strictly daytime event, you still need to be prepared for nighttime. The rally may end near dusk and unexpected storm clouds or simply some miscalculations can put you in a situation where driving lights will help you pick out important landmarks. It is a perfect excuse to install some Cibies or Marchals.

Interior lighting is also important. You never know when a late starting position or a slowed rally due to unusual weather can make it very dark inside the car—darker, in fact, than outside. If you have to spend the last hour or so of the rally trying to read instructions, you are in real trouble. It is wise to install navigation lights of the type that are shielded so that the navigator can read the instructions without distracting the driver. And keep a flashlight on board with fresh batteries, just in case all else fails.

All veteran rallyists agree that a reader board (or centerboard) is the most important single piece of navigational equipment. It can be anything from a clipboard to a sophisticated device available through many rally publications. The more elaborate ones have counters and/or stopwatches. No matter which kind you use, it should be mounted between driver and navigator so both can see. The board will eliminate a lot of unnecessary conversation, and that is advisable.

No driver can remember all the instructions, so the easier you can make it, the better. During times when the navigator can afford to take attention away from the immediate situation, he can write notes on small pieces of self-adhesive white paper, available in rolls at most stationery stores. Then, just before the particular instruction is due, the navigator can stick that note on the dash, right in the driver's line of sight. The driver must be able to read it easily and quickly read without looking away from the route for too long. Print clearly. And large. Then, when the note is no longer pertinent, the navigator can rip it off and replace it with a more current one.

Make sure the odometer is working properly and accurately. Check it against other cars and, if you are fortunate enough to have a test section of highway, use it. If you need to have the odometer recalibrated, do so. It can spell the difference between winning and losing. The driver should operate the odometer, changing it when necessary to keep track of instructions. If the navigator attempts to do it, he will get in the way of the driver's elbows and slow things down.

It doesn't matter if you are a direct descendant of Magellan—you still need a compass. In the heat of battle, it is easy to lose your bearings, and if you get lost, you can write it all off. Well, winning anyway. But if you do get lost, don't give up. There will be others—many others—who get lost, and if you get back on course quickly, you may still have a chance of taking home a trophy.

If you *do* get off course, quickly determine on your road map exactly where you are. With the compass, you might be able to find a quicker route back to the rally course. For example, instead of turning around and retracing your goof-up, you might find that by going south a mile or so you can intersect the proper route. Of course, it helps to know which way is south.

Buy a good dash-mounted compass. You will be surprised at how many times you will use it in nonrally situations.

It is wise, in fact, to be overequipped. Don't overlook anything that you can afford to buy and that the organizers allow in your particular class. And be sure you are proficient in its operation. Having the most sophisticated equipment this side of NASA won't help a bit if you are not familiar with its use. Practice at home until you've got it down pat.

The use of a *color code* for route instructions will be immensely helpful. For example, you might use a yellow magic marker circle around each pause and a blue one around course and mileage markers. Use whatever colors turn you on, but memorize the code so you can decipher it at a glance. Most rallies issue two sets of instructions, one for driver and one for navigator, so make sure you mark each set. This, too, can eliminate a lot of conversation. The navigator can simply say "Yellow thirty-seven" or "Blue one-point-one," which the driver can interpret to mean a change in average speed to 37 mph or a change in course coming up in 1.1 miles.

The navigator must keep a thorough log. This is imperative. It not only helps you keep a running "feel" of the rally, but you can fall back on the log if you get lost. And it is a helpful reference for after the rally, a guide to figuring out traps for the next rally. The navigator will probably want to write the mileage between each speed change segment and between checkpoints directly on the route instructions, along with the calculated time. This is an easy way to develop a log sheet system that works; it also provides an invaluable device for study later on to see exactly where you might have lost time and points.

The log system provides the quickest routine for "getting back on course" that you can have. Obviously, if you got lost, you didn't follow the instructions properly so reversing the route instructions isn't going to help a great deal. But if you can refer to your log, and compare it with the rally instructions, you can probably find your mistake. Stop the car immediately and figure it out. There is no use compounding the error.

As accurately as possible, estimate the lost time. Perhaps you can make up some of it.

Devise convenient holders and mounting devices for all of your rally equipment. Make sure it is easily accessible to the person who needs to see or operate it. Properly mounted equipment frees your hands to use other equipment, and it eliminates bothersome fussing around when you need to find something. By the same token, keep any spare equipment handy in the back seat so that when necessary you can grab it quickly. If you have spare timepieces, make sure they are wound and zeroed in. Have more sharpened pencils than you can ever use, as well as felt markers in all colors so you can quickly mark instructions in your own color code that you might have overlooked.

Approach

Once you have your equipment and are proficient in its use, you must work out the proper approach to everything.

Read the generals (general instructions) until you can nearly recite them by rote. Then read them a few more times. And this means *both* navigator and driver. If the driver completely understands the generals, all the navigator has to do is give accurate and concise instructions and the driver will understand exactly what to do.

But don't depend on memory. Keep the generals handy and color-coded, and keep the stick-on notes rolling. Underline each term on the generals that applies to the road. You may want to circle an entire paragraph or simply underscore the first line, but do whatever is necessary to call important clues to quick attention. This completely eliminates rereading through an entire paragraph, much of which may be cutesy stuff to make the instructions read well. Chaff.

Some seasoned rallyists even scissor out the important instructions on one set of generals and tape it all together in a more concise, logical order. This certainly eliminates a lot of unnecessary reading, because most rally instructions tend to lean toward the creative in wording.

Driver and navigator should familiarize themselves with all of the scoring penalties. It is good to know exactly how much it will cost you in points if you are late at a checkpoint or if your average speed is way below what it should be. Or how much it will cost you if you must speed to make up for lost time. Such knowledge enables you to place the proper importance on the various aspects of the rally.

Saab has been described by many as the best winter car in the world. Here at an English winter rally, one displays the form that earned it its reputation.

Gamesmanship

Studying the rallymaster is probably the first step in gamesmanship. If you know the style of the rally and of the person who put it together, you will have a pretty good idea of any gimmicks that might be written into the event. You will know if this particular rallymaster uses traps or if he plays it straight down the line. Keep files on each rally, because most rallyists agree that once a rallymaster adopts a particular style, he usually doesn't vary too much from that style. It is probably the image he wishes to have.

The best way to develop a style and a feel for the sport is to learn as much as you can from an expert. It is like going to a driving school. If possible, run a rally or two with an expert driver or navigator. You can learn more in one rally about equipment and driving than you could in a dozen rallies on your own. There is no replacement for experience, and if you can call on somebody else's, you will be way ahead of the game.

8

Driving in Rain and Snow

Mother Nature isn't entirely sold on competitive automotive events; otherwise it wouldn't rain so often on SCCA and IMSA races. Some rallies, of course, *depend* on bad weather conditions to make them interesting. If you don't ski in winter you have to rally. That's why snow was invented. So if you are faced with racing or rallying on a slippery surface, it is imperative to know what your car is going to do under such conditions, and, more particularly, what *you* are going to do. What works on ice, for the most part, works even better on rain-soaked tracks. And certainly on the open highway.

Front-wheel drive cars are usually better in icy and wet conditions, and Saab is considered by expert winter drivers to be the best of the best, so we asked Lennert Lonnegren of Saab-Scandia of America to give us some advice.

"Every car model has its specific behavior on the road," says Lonnegren. "Factors affecting the road behavior of a car include its size, weight, weight distribution, wheel suspension, location of the center of gravity, and even the styling of the body. Under slippery conditions, the behavior of a car is primarily dependent on the location of the driving wheels.

"Our advice and hints apply to all cars—not merely the Saab models we have used for the photographs. But this general applicability excludes special maneuvers, such as handling a skid.

"If a driver is to be truly safe, he must know the behavior of his car in all situations, particularly under slippery road conditions, when the least error may have disastrous consequences. Extra care is essential when cornering, braking, and accelerating. Training in these and other typical winter motoring situations can be gained on special skid tracks or on a cleared frozen lake. A driver who has become thoroughly acquainted with his car and has learned to handle it in all situations is a safer and more relaxed driver. He can then concentrate more on the traffic and thus avoid difficult situations.

"Training in driving on a slippery surface is advisable at least once a year. And also when changing over to a different car. The best approach is to refresh one's memory just before winter has clamped down in earnest."

Speed and Ice

Regardless of whether the road is covered by snow, ice, or slush, one rule is paramount: Always drive at a road speed that matches the condition of the road surface.

A seemingly clear and dry road may have a treacherous covering of black ice. Bridges and overpasses, which are also cooled from below, are particularly dangerous. In such areas, high speeds may be lethal.

At the transition between a city and the countryside, the road may suddenly change from a perfectly dry surface to a sheet of ice. The driver usually won't notice the change in the condition of the surface, and even experienced drivers may be unable to foresee the sudden change. If a constant speed is maintained on long stretches of road, dangerous situations may occur due to sudden variations in the road surface and thus in the grip of the tires.

In a nutshell, always allow a little extra time before setting out on a winter journey and always drive at a speed slightly below that which you are certain you can handle safely. If you have an opportunity to find out the conditions of the roads, do so and adjust your speed accordingly. Take particular care if the road is icy or covered with new snow and when the visibility is impaired by falling snow, fog, or darkness. Bear in mind that the general speed limits are not recommended cruising speeds. During the winter, the legally permissible speed is often too high to be safe.

Avoid Jerky Maneuvers

Jerky maneuvers are the most common reason a driver loses control of the car under slippery conditions. Sudden acceleration on a slippery road may cause wheel spin, and all lateral stabilizing effect of the driving wheels will be lost. On a car with front-wheel drive, this will cause the car to continue basically straight ahead, regardless of all steering efforts of the driver. The front of the car may even start skidding sideways, depending on the camber of the road, cross winds, or the like. On a car with rear-wheel drive, the loss of lateral stabilizing effect will usually induce the rear wheels to skid.

Sudden braking and locking of the wheels will have about the same effect as wheel spin. The locked wheels will lose all lateral stabilizing effect, the car will not respond to the steering wheel, and it will skid, possibly sideways, in the direction in which the road slopes.

Sudden turning of the steering wheel may also cause problems. The car may not respond immediately to the steering wheel. The front wheels may very well start to skid sideways on the slippery surface. When the wheels finally grip the road, the car may turn so suddenly that the rear wheels start to skid instead.

There is only one solution to all of these problems—avoid all sudden maneuvers.

Many racers unfortunately labor under the misapprehension that skidding a car through a turn offers increased speed. Hollywood promotes this view by dramatizing their productions with screaming-tire scenes. Rally drivers often approach a turn too fast and must skid through. But the fastest rally drivers take their turns as smoothly as possible—without skidding.

This misconception about skidding is regrettable. It may lead to many unnecessary risks in traffic. Experienced rally drivers do everything possible to avoid situations in which the car skids, even though it may be permissible on a closed circuit. In any case, they do their best to avoid skids on public roads, where such driving should be classified as an error in judgment.

How to Avoid Skidding

Skidding—in which the front wheels, the rear wheels, or the entire car moves laterally—is one of the most dangerous motoring situations. On road *or* track. Skidding is usually a result of too-high speeds—possibly combined with sudden turning of the steering wheel, heavy acceleration, hard braking, or brain fade.

Rear-wheel skid.

Driving in Rain and Snow

6. REAR-WHEEL SKID

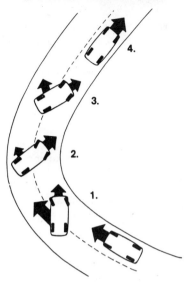

Skidding is best avoided by slowing down in good time before a turn and then taking the turn at a steady throttle. This is the technique employed by rally drivers in fast and safe cornering.

But if your speed is too high as you enter a turn, don't panic, don't brake heavily, and don't jerk the steering wheel.

A Rear-Wheel Skid

If the rear wheels of your car should accidentally skid, here is the best way to regain control. For cars with front-wheel drive:

1. Steer in the same direction as the rear wheels are skidding.
2. Depress the clutch on a car with a manual gearbox or take your foot off the accelerator pedal if the car has automatic transmission. With automatics, don't try to move the selector to neutral unless you are certain of finding it immediately.
3. Wait until the rear wheels have stopped skidding and then steer the car gently back, so that the front wheels point straight ahead when the rear wheels are back on course.
4. Release the clutch and depress the accelerator gently so that the engine speed matches the road speed and continue to accelerate gently. Note: There is no real risk of the car skidding in the opposite direction.

For cars with rear-wheel drive:

1. Steer in the same direction as the rear wheels are skidding.
2. Depress the clutch on a car with a manual gearbox or take your foot off the accelerator pedal if the car has automatic transmission.
3. Wait until the rear wheels have stopped skidding and then steer the car gently back, so that the front wheels point straight ahead when the rear wheels are back on course.
4. Be prepared to have the rear wheels start to skid in the opposite direction. Training and extremely gentle movement of the steering wheel are essential to prevent this more difficult skid. When you feel that the car is on its way to straightening up, return the steering wheel to normal position. But make sure you don't overcorrect the first skid. That might cause a rear-wheel skid in the opposite direction.
5. Release the clutch and depress the accelerator gently so that the engine speed matches the road speed and continue to accelerate gently.

A Front-Wheel Skid

A front-wheel skid is also dangerous and, since it is far less common than a rear-wheel skid, it is often considered to be even more dangerous. But nothing could be further from the truth. A front-wheel skid is easier to correct and there is no risk whatever of the car skidding in the opposite

7. FRONT-WHEEL SKID

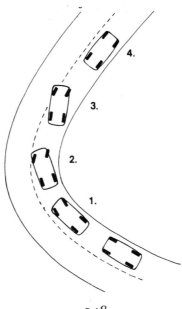

Front-wheel skid.

direction. If you have entered a curve so fast or have accelerated or braked so heavily that the front wheels have more or less lost their steering capacity, the situation is very easy to correct. Regardless of whether the car has front-wheel or rear-wheel drive, your best way out is as follows:

1. Don't move the steering wheel.
2. Depress the clutch on a car with a manual gearbox or take your foot off the accelerator pedal if the car has automatic transmission.
3. Wait for the front wheels to grip again. Since the wheels are skidding sideways they exert a certain braking effect. As soon as the speed has dropped off enough for the road surface or the curvature of the turn, the car will start to steer again.
4. When the front wheels have gripped again, steer the wheels carefully to make up for what you have lost in the skid.
5. Release the clutch and depress the accelerator gently so that the engine speed matches the road speed and continue to accelerate gently.

There is no risk at all of the car starting to skid in the opposite direction.

Wet Ice

If you examine the track of a locked wheel on ice, you will notice a shiny surface. This shiny surface has formed as follows:

When a wheel is braked, heat will be generated by the friction between the tire and the road surface. The surface of the ice will then melt, becoming a lubricating film of water. The locked wheel will have a longer braking distance than a wheel which exerts a braking effort while continuing to roll. A typical example of this situation is the highly polished ice at road intersections. Car after car brakes with locked wheels, and this renders the surface extremely slippery. Bear this in mind when approaching a road crossing. Brake early—and without locking the wheels.

Aquaplaning

Once you experience aquaplaning (or hydroplaning), you'll never forget it. The car becomes completely uncontrollable. It cannot be steered and it cannot be braked. Aquaplaning is caused by the tires literally losing contact with the road surface.

When a tire is running on a wet surface, the water must be expelled toward the rear and to the sides through the tire tread to keep the tire in contact with the road surface. The better the tread pattern, the less risk of aquaplaning.

If the speed of the car or the depth of the water increases, a wedge of water will first form in front of the tire. Time is too short for this wedge to be "squeezed out" and it therefore stays in front of the tire, although not yet affecting its steering and braking capacity.

The weapons against aquaplaning are primarily good tires and low speeds. With worn tires, aquaplaning may start at speeds as low as 35mph. The wider the tire, the greater the risk of aquaplaning. More water must be drained away from a wide tire than from a narrow one.

Grooves in the road surface, caused primarily by studded tires, also increase the risk of aquaplaning. On a slushy surface, "slush-planing" may occur, and this is even more dangerous than aquaplaning, since it may start at very low speeds.

If you experience aquaplaning or slush-planing, don't brake and don't jerk the steering wheel. That would only make things worse. Depress the clutch, let the car roll and lose speed, and wait until the tires grip the road again.

Follow the Tracks

Dense traffic on a snow-covered road will create tracks which may be several inches deep. Although the tracks are usually the most slippery part of the road, they are still the safest place to be. As long as you stay in the tracks and keep well behind the car in front of you, you may feel fairly safe. Problems will arise only when you leave the tracks and venture into the deep snow, to pass another car, for example.

If the wheels refuse to "cross" the mound of snow, give up the attempt and wait for a better opportunity. Otherwise you run the risk of turning the steering wheel too much, and the car will skid when the front wheels grip.

Once in the deeper snow, be prepared for the car to "flounder," leaving you unable to accelerate past the car in front.

To avoid a skid, steer the car toward the mound of snow at the smallest possible angle. And make sure your speed is slightly faster than the remainder of the traffic just before you start passing.

Braking

One of the most important reasons for training regularly on a slippery surface is to learn the correct braking technique.

On a skid pad or ice track, you can learn the feather-light footwork necessary for the wheels to transmit maximum braking effort without locking. If the wheels should lock, the braking effort and the directional stability of the car will be impaired. And you probably will skid sideways.

Never "slam on" the brakes in a critical situation. Apply the brakes fairly hard—at most so that the wheels lock for an instant—and then ease off (but don't take your foot off) the brake pedal so that the wheels are almost at the point of locking. This will give you the best braking effect and the car will stay on course.

Using a Snow Bank

The worst conceivable situation for a motorist is seeing an obstacle on the road and knowing that he has no chance of stopping in time. Fortunately, winter usually offers the best alternative to a collision. The roadside snow bank can be used as a brake. Instead of crashing into the obstacle with locked or almost locked wheels, steer at the smallest possible angle into the bank of snow at the side of the road. The side of the car will scrape along the bank, reducing the speed. If the bank is soft, the car may emerge entirely undamaged. Even if, as is more usual, the hard-packed snow causes scratches or minor dents, this is nothing compared with what would happen if you were to drive straight into another car. Steering into the snow bank is usually less dangerous and less expensive than steering into the First National Bank.

Controlling Your Vision

Motorists often find it difficult to control their vision. Though this is not specifically related to driving in slippery conditions, it may be worth mentioning here.

Always remember to set your vision as far ahead of the car as possible. Your eyes will not be unnecessarily strained and you will have a better opportunity to see situations as they develop.

Never look into the headlights of oncoming cars when driving at night. Your eyes are naturally drawn to the strong light sources, but do your best to keep your vision toward the edge of the road. Your night vision will be greatly improved, as will your night driving.

9

Tune-up for Performance and Economy

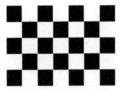

Unless you run across the exception to a long-standing rule, you may never find a *race car* mechanic who will help you keep your performance machine in top form. And, even if you do find one who will give you hints, you might not want to put too much stock in them. I mean, why would he give away the really good secrets it may have taken him years to learn himself?

It becomes, then, a matter of taking good, solid highway practices and refining them. The modifications we discussed earlier are relatively easy to maintain and don't require all that different an approach from highway maintenance. If, along the way, you do run across a willing race car mechanic, so much the better. But, until then, you should have little trouble keeping your car in top running form.

What is probably more important to the average performance-oriented driver is knowing *what* to do and being able to perform the tasks personally. It can save about $25 an hour. Besides that, most people who are interested enough to want to improve their own or their car's performance also enjoy knowing more about the machine. There's a satisfaction in keeping it in really top-notch condition.

Start with a service manual for your car—not the owner's manual that comes with the car, but the hefty manual you can buy from your automotive dealer or from some automotive parts stores. The manual will give you precise instructions on how to do every task necessary to keep your car running, from the simplest maneuvers to major overhauls. There are few special tools necessary, but the manual will describe any you should have.

Aside from screwdrivers, combination wrenches, pliers, and the like, you should have a set of feeler gauges for gapping spark plugs and points (if your car has points) and a timing light. If the car is not equipped with a tachometer, a combination meter that measures rpm as well as dwell would be helpful. If you use the tach on the car, make sure it is accurate by checking it against a borrowed tune-up tach.

The performance machine, or even the finely tuned road car, requires far more attention than the service procedures suggested by the manufacturer. It is this near-constant tinkering that has set the enthusiast apart from the commuter for many years. Otherwise God wouldn't have invented the MG.

Aside from the general good practice of keeping a close eye on the condition of plug wires, distributor caps, hoses, belts, and fuel lines, you should retain a written record of exactly when the plugs and oil were changed and the tires rotated. It seems a simple thing to remember, but you would be surprised at how quickly you forget whether you performed the task at 13,000 miles or 15,000. Write it down on a small pad, which should be kept in the glove box. Breakerless ignitions have eliminated points and have greatly increased spark plug life, but it is still wise to change plugs more frequently than the manufacturer recommends. For one thing, a perfectly tuned car will give you enough of an increase in fuel economy to easily pay for the early replacement.

Unless you have bolted on, say, a new Holley carburetor, or another good after-market carb, there probably isn't an adjustment on your carburetor in the first place. If the original-equipment carb gets out of whack, you simply buy a new one. It's a little thing the EPA and carburetor manufacturers like a lot.

So, with the advent of breakerless ignition systems and nonadjustable carburetors, the old task of tuning-up a car should be simpler than in the good ol' days before Washington got involved. But today's severe limitations make it even more important that the few adjustable parts stay *perfectly* adjusted. And if, along the way, you can fudge a little, well, so much the better.

One thing most drivers overlook in the regular maintenance category is the braking system. Almost as important to performance as "go" is "whoa." Being able to stop quickly and efficiently as well as to corner properly is vital both to the performance of the car and the capability of the driver. Brakes are not just devices for preventing everything from becoming a "drive-in."

Every tune-up should include a careful inspection of the car's braking system. You should thoroughly check brake lines and wheel and master cylinders for leaks. Most people check the fluid reservoir from time to time; and if it isn't dangerously low, they let it go at that. But you should inspect lines and every part of the system to the point of completely wiping clean the lines, particularly the major bends, to see if there is even the slightest leak. If there is a damp spot anywhere, check to see if it is brake fluid. If you can't tell, have someone depress the brake pedal while you watch to see if any fluid appears on the cleaned area.

Most often leaks appear on flexible lines or at connections, and the part can be easily replaced or the connection tightened.

Now comes the part that most drivers don't know: Brake fluid should be changed regularly, once a year under normal conditions, more often under severe driving conditions. For one thing, the fluid absorbs moisture, and this alters its effectiveness. The relatively new silicone fluids resist moisture more than other types, but almost any good, reliable fluid will do. Just don't buy a cut-rate brand. Good brake fluid is not that expensive, so it is no place to cut corners. And—unlike aspirin which is supposed to be basically the same, regardless of cost—good brake fluid, as compared to the cheap stuff, can save you a lot of headaches.

If you use your car in competition, you will want to change often, maybe every couple of races, because fluid that has absorbed any moisture at all will boil more quickly and, from a performance viewpoint, that's as critical as overheated linings.

What follows in this chapter can be used on road or track cars.

The Importance of Oil

The thought that recommended oil changes are for the complete benefit of the oil companies is as wrong as the belief that racing tires benefit only Goodyear.

The American Petroleum Institute recommends that motor oil be drained at regular intervals, at least as frequently as prescribed in the car owner's operating manual. Because mileage and time for optimum oil drain intervals vary according to type of driving and environment, car owners should pay particular attention to the car manufacturers' recommendations prescribed for severe service. Severe service includes very short trips, extensive idling, stop-and-go driving, cold-weather operation, dusty conditions, extended high speeds, heavy loads, and trailer towing—conditions frequently encountered by a majority of motorists.

Because oil technology has made great strides in recent years, the motor oils of today are capable of protecting engine parts and prolonging engine life better than ever before. To obtain this protection the car owner must:

· Use an oil of the recommended service classification.
· Select the proper SAE oil viscosity.
· Change the oil at proper intervals.

Just as oil changes are desirable at regular intervals, it is equally important that oil filters be changed in accordance with the car manufacturers' recommendations.

It should be pointed out that oil change recommendations for current-model cars are not retroactive and do not alter the recommendations made for earlier models. This is important because in recent years oil change intervals have generally been extended. Applying such schedules to older cars could lead to serious problems.

Oil is another relatively inexpensive item, particularly if you perform your own oil and filter changes. You can shop around and find good oil at an inexpensive price. But "good" is the key word. Usually the automobile manufacturer recommends several in the owner's manual. Use one of them or one of the top brands available at most outlets. Oil is no place to cut corners.

Len Manley, of Valvoline, had this to say about the new, smaller engine: "Through the years, the general trend in engine design has been to limit the physical size of the engine while increasing its useful output. Until about 1970, this increased output was obtained mainly through higher compression ratios. This resulted in higher cylinder pressures and temperatures which required the motor oil to do a more efficient job of minimizing engine deposit formation. The higher combustion pressures also placed greater loads on rings and bearings, making lubrication of these parts more difficult.

"The adoption in recent years of progressively stringent exhaust emission controls has reversed the trend to higher compression ratios. These ratios have declined to provide for the use of lower octane, unleaded gasoline. This became necessary when catalytic converters were installed on most 1975-model cars to meet the strict exhaust emission limits.

"These changing trends, along with changes in engine design, have made new and more severe demands on lubricating oil. Engine modifications for emission control, such as positive crankcase ventilation (PCV), exhaust gas recirculation (EGR), spark retard and leaner air-fuel ratios, as well as the increasing use of power accessories (air-conditioning, power steering), have resulted in higher under-hood temperatures and in more severe engine operating conditions. All of these factors have added to the burden that the lubricating oils must carry in order to maintain satisfactory engine performance."

Tune-up for Performance and Economy

To get more fuel mixture into—and therefore more power out of—the cylinders, the "breathing capacity" of engines has been increased by using larger valves that open and close more rapidly. These require stiffer valve springs. Cams have been narrowed to increase engine compactness.

These design changes have not only affected engine performance, but also have increased the loads on cams, valve lifters, push rods, rocker arms, and valve stem tips. Prevention of rapid wear, scuffing, surface fatigue, and flaking became more difficult. Cam noses were sometimes worn away, necessitating expensive camshaft replacement.

The temperatures and types of service under which an engine is operated vary markedly. Moderate-speed driving on short trips, or stop-and-go driving in traffic, uses only a fraction of the available engine power. Because the cooling systems must be capable of meeting the cooling requirements of the engine at high speeds, they may overcool the engine during short-trip driving. In such light-duty service, engines and motor oils warm up slowly and often fail to reach proper operating temperatures.

Under these conditions, automatic chokes will provide the engine with the rich air-fuel mixture it needs to operate smoothly at cold temperatures, but this richness will result in incomplete combustion. Soot and partially oxidized hydrocarbons undergo further oxidation in the crankcase, forming sludge and varnish deposits. These may clog oil screens or plug oil rings, interfering with oil circulation and control, or they may cause hydraulic valve lifters and valves to stick. Corrosive acids are formed, and they cause wear on piston rings, cylinders, and occasionally, piston skirts. Steam from combustion condenses on cylinder walls and drains into the crankcase. Water, often in combination with acidic gases, may cause valve lifters to rust and stick. It may also create rust deposits on piston pins, rocker arm shafts, and valve stems. Liquid fuel that leaks past the piston rings dilutes the oil and reduces its lubricating value. These are some of the effects of engine operation at cold temperatures.

"As a car is driven," says Manley, "the level of contaminants in the motor oil is constantly increasing. Since combustion products are continually being formed and picked up by the oil, it becomes more and more difficult for the oil to protect and lubricate the engine.

"As an example, the additives which disperse sludge-forming materials and prevent rust and corrosion are used up in performing their function, much as a cake of soap is used up as it does its job. When this additive depletion reaches a certain point, the oil can no longer do its job and must be changed.

"The rate at which contamination and additive depletion occur depends on a number of variables. One of these is driving habits, which vary greatly and have a direct effect on the useful life of the oil. Other factors include the precision of ignition and carburetion adjustments, air-cleaner service, and the mechanical condition of the engine. The latter is often reflected in the amount of blowby to the crankcase. Blowby increases as the wear condition of the engine deteriorates and is a significant contributor to oil contamination."

Spark Plugs and Ignition

Prompted by efforts to combat air pollution and improve fuel economy, engines and ignition systems have passed through rapid stages of development in recent years.

Rotary combustion and stratified charge engines are but two new concepts that have found their way into the world-motoring market. The automotive industry is now into the second stage of electronic ignition systems with such sophisticated equipment as Ford's EEC (Electronic Engine Control System), GM's EST-MISAR (Electronic Spark Timing Microprocessed Sensing Automatic Regulation), and Chrysler Corporation's ELB (Electronic Lean Burn).

The efficiency of any engine, indeed its ability to operate at all, is directly dependent on the ignition qualities of a small component which has no moving parts—the spark plug. And the spark plug can be blamed for many performance and fuel-economy problems, according to Tony Mougey of the Champion Spark Plug Company.

"A Champion nationwide test program of nearly six thousand cars pointed out the fact that almost seventy-nine percent of all cars checked had deficiencies adversely affecting fuel economy, emissions, or performance," Mougey explained.

"Maintenance neglect is expensive to car owners. Under-maintained vehicles cost millions of dollars in unnecessary fuel bills and waste our precious energy resources. In addition, lack of proper care takes its toll in starting failures, inferior performance, and poor air quality.

"The information obtained in our test programs demonstrates to the motorist the benefits of a tune-up in maintaining vehicles for improved fuel economy and low exhaust emissions."

Conventional Ignition

In a conventional ignition system, the voltage necessary to fire the spark plug is developed when the contact points in the distributor are opened, interrupting a primary current flow through an induction coil.

The system must be capable of supplying the amount of voltage necessary to create a spark across the electrode gap at the firing tip of the spark plug. This requires a considerable "ignition reserve" to take care of normal wear factors of both spark plugs and ignition system components.

Simply stated, ignition reserve is the difference in kilovolts between how much the ignition system can produce (voltage available), and how much it takes for the coil to discharge a spark across the plug gap (voltage required).

There are several factors that can decrease ignition reserve, causing a decline in performance and an increase in emissions. Worn or defective ignition system components decrease voltage available. Worn spark plugs, reversed coil polarity, damaged plug wires, and retarded ignition timing increase voltage required. These are but a few of the more obvious problems.

Modern oscilloscopes offer a quick and accurate means of measuring voltage levels during actual engine operation. On a screen, they produce patterns that illustrate traces of both voltage available and voltage required. This method of testing is extremely useful in gauging the condition of the ignition system and spark plugs.

Electronic Ignition

The function of the electronic ignition system is the same as its conventional counterpart—to produce a high-voltage spark and distribute it at the proper time to fire the spark plugs.

Though the distributor and a few related components are similar to those in a conventional system, there are several areas where they differ. Gone are the breaker points that burn and pit and the distributor cam rubbing block that wears, bringing about changes in ignition timing. They've been replaced by a magnetic impulse system and advanced electronics that require only a minimal amount of maintenance.

Regular ignition system maintenance has been minimized to inspection of all wiring and connections, the distributor cap, rotor, and ignition coil. The need for ignition service continues to exist—only the degree of inspection or correction has changed.

The role and environment of the spark plug has not changed, however. High-voltage discharges, chemical attack, and high combustion temperatures will continue to dictate regular plug change intervals to maintain optimum economy and performance.

Cross Fire

Cross fire is the common trade term used to identify induction leakage at the spark plug wire. This condition will often occur when ignition cables are grouped closely together and run in parallel paths for some distance. Engine roughness is a primary clue (when the ignition system and spark plugs are known to be in good operating condition), and can lead to damaging pre-ignition or detonation.

Some technicians believe cross fire is directly traceable to a breakdown in cable insulation or defective cable construction. Not so! Rather, it is caused by the strong, magnetic field that surrounds any high-tension conductor. Because of this phenomenon, the cable carrying the high voltage tends to induce voltage into an adjacent cable, thus firing one of the other plugs "out of time."

Cross fire is most likely to occur between consecutive firing cylinders when these cylinders are located close together in the engine block.

Coil Polarity

Hard starting and a high-speed miss are reasons to suspect that ignition polarity has been reversed. This problem is due to improperly connected primary leads at the ignition coil. As a rule of thumb, remember that coil polarity should always be *negative* at the spark plug terminal, as this decreases voltage required to fire the plug—under some conditions, as much as 40 percent. The primary lead from the distributor should be connected to the negative (−) terminal on the coil. This applies to all cars with a 12-volt, negative ground battery.

To check coil polarity, use an oscilloscope. If the trace pattern is upside down, the polarity is incorrect. If the system has been operating for some time with the wrong polarity, check the spark plugs. Evidence of "dishing" on the underside of the ground electrode is a good clue.

Dwell Angle and Ignition Timing

Basic ignition timing (on conventional ignition systems) is directly affected by dwell angle. Spacing the point gap too wide decreases the dwell angle and advances the ignition spark. If the point gap is too narrow, dwell angle will increase and retard the ignition spark. Whenever contact points are replaced or dwell angle is adjusted, ignition timing should be reset to the manufacturer's specifications.

Every engine has a point at which it can be timed to deliver its maximum power and economy, and you may have to experiment to determine this point. But keep in mind that a great over-advance in timing may result in more problems than power. Champion points out that an 8-degree advance in timing of the average engine results in only a 2 percent power increase. But it greatly increases the spark plug temperature.

A decal listing all of the tune-up data is firmly attached to the splash shield or some other accessible place under the hood of all vehicles built since 1968. The decal lists the correct initial engine timing, idle speed, and idle exhaust mixtures, as well as other important tune-up data.

New contacts for some distributors may be adjusted with reasonable accuracy using a clean feeler gauge.

Because emission control systems for late-model cars require precise distributor adjustments, car manufacturers recommend that the contact gap be set with a dwell meter. Used contacts must always be set with a dwell meter.

Too little gap causes excessive dwell and late timing, but too much gap causes insufficient dwell and early timing. Remember, spark occurs and the air-fuel mixture starts to burn the instant the points begin opening.

You should also remember that one degree of dwell change will result in one degree of spark timing change.

With the engine at normal operation temperature, disconnect the distributor advance diaphragm vacuum tube or tubes and plug the end of the tubes (a wooden golf tee makes an excellent plug). Adjust the timing to factory specifications. Timing should be adjusted after distributor contact dwell is set.

Changing Spark Plugs

Because of the operational makeup of the conventional, breaker-type ignition system, a 10,000-mile plug change recommendation has been, and will continue to be, a reasonable and realistic policy. This recommendation is not based on the fact that spark plugs actually "wear out," in the strictest sense, after 10,000 miles of service. This figure represents a point beyond which worn plugs are likely to misfire during the peak voltage demands of sudden acceleration. Misfire will result in a loss of power and economy. Also, worn spark plugs contribute to starting failures, a problem that is compounded by wet or cold weather.

Electronic ignition systems, as efficient as they are, do not change the environment in which the spark plug must operate. High combustion temperatures, chemical attack, and high-voltage discharges will continue to determine the service life of the plug. Periodic replacement will always be necessary to maintain maximum economy and performance. A good replacement policy for cars with electronic ignition systems is at least once a year.

In heavy traffic, on short trips, and for other low-speed driving, modern engines use only a small percentage of their available power. As a result, engine temperatures remain low, and various products of combustion accumulate as deposits on the firing end of the spark plugs. These deposits are often conductive and can short the spark, causing misfire.

When old plugs go, the entire set should be replaced. If you install only two or three new plugs at one time, you will probably have to replace the rest in short order. With a "bit by bit" replacement, a motorist never realizes the full advantage of new-plug performance and economy. A chain is no stronger than its weakest link, and an engine is no "newer" than its oldest plug.

Regular plug replacement and proper ignition servicing give added benefits in better performance, economy, and faster starting.

To remove a spark plug wire from the spark plug, gently twist the connection at the plug. This action breaks the seal and makes the connection easy to remove. Don't tug or jerk on the wire.

If you suspect a bad wire or fouled plug, the engine can be checked by the rpm drop method. With a tachometer connected to the engine, disconnect one spark plug wire at a time and carefully note the rpm drop and engine roughness. A bad wire or spark plug will indicate little or no rpm drop.

After their normal service life, one or more of the plugs may be a little difficult to loosen. Allowing the engine ample cool-down time will facilitate plug removal. The use of a penetrating oil is also recommended if the plug appears to be dangerously tight. Apply steady pressure with a plug wrench until the plug loosens. Before removing the plug, blow from the port area any dirt that might be present to prevent it from falling into the combustion chamber.

If the plug appears to be overly tight when removed by hand, there may be carbon collecting in the threaded area of the cylinder head. This condition is more common in older engines. The threads should be cleaned with a chaser tool, and the seat wiped clean to assure good seat contact before installing a new plug.

Install the new plug finger-tight, and complete the installation with a plug wrench. A gasket-type plug will require about one-quarter turn to effect a gas-tight seal. Tapered-seat plugs do not use gaskets and require about one-sixteenth turn.

Tune-up for Performance and Economy

Examining the Plugs

Close examination of spark plugs can offer clues to the fitness of any engine, I learned in interviews with Champion Spark Plug engineers. The examination will be especially informative if you keep the plugs in order according to their cylinder location. Their position in the engine may help locate a problem that might otherwise go undetected. Finding only one plug overheated might indicate an intake manifold leak near the location of the particular cylinder. If the overheated plug is the second of two adjacent, consecutively firing plugs, it might signal cross fire.

Two fouled plugs located adjacent to each other might mean a blown head gasket. Cooling system problems may surface in the form of overheated plugs, possibly localized if blockages occur in certain areas of the engine. One oil-fouled plug should indicate poor oil control in a particular cylinder.

These are only hints as to the importance of keeping the plugs in order as they are removed. This procedure will make diagnosis even more effective.

The spark plug is a remarkable product of modern engineering knowhow. Because it is positioned in the combustion chamber, it is readily exposed to the extremes of hot and cold temperatures, is subject to the attack of chemicals from fuels and oils in a corrosive atmosphere, and must never miss a beat under the hammering pressures produced by the piston.

The atmosphere within which the spark plug operates can be determined by simply removing the plug and reading the firing end—a procedure which has now become an exact science. Compared to its new condition, the spark plug firing end will have changed in color and may be coated or encrusted with a variety of telltale compounds that may or may not affect the performance of the engine. Close examination of spark plugs can give clues as to the fitness of an engine and sometimes expose a problem that normally might go unnoticed.

Heat Range

Possibly the first step in reading the firing end of a used spark plug is determining whether it is in the correct heat range or not. The term *heat range* refers to the temperature scale within which the spark plug operates.

A spark plug must transfer heat from its firing tip into the cylinder head and cooling medium. The rate of this heat transfer is largely dependent upon the length of the insulator nose. A "cold"-type plug has a short insulator nose and transfers heat into the cylinder head very rapidly. In comparison, a "hot"-type plug has a longer insulator nose and transfers heat more slowly.

Normal (courtesy Champion Spark Plug Company).

The color of the insulator nose should be a light brown to grayish color with minimal electrode erosion indicating correct spark plug heat range and a "healthy" engine. If this plug is to be reinstalled, it should be properly cleaned first, and the electrodes filed and reset to the recommended gap. If it has been in service for over 10,000 miles and is being replaced, spark plugs of the same heat range should be used. Example: Remove Champion RJ-12Y, replace with new RJ-12Y.

Oil Fouling

Oil-fouled plugs indicate that an excessive quantity of oil is entering the combustion chamber. In an engine with high mileage, the piston rings or

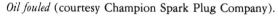

Oil fouled (courtesy Champion Spark Plug Company).

cylinder walls may be excessively worn. In overhead valve engines, oil may seep past the valve guides. If the fuel pump diaphragm is ruptured, a quantity of oil may enter the combustion chamber, resulting in oil-fouled plugs.

"Break-in" fouling in new engines may occur before normal oil control is achieved. In new or recently overhauled engines, such oil-fouled plugs can be degreased, cleaned, and reinstalled.

In an effort to burn off and subsequently control excessive oil deposits, a hot spark plug has often been substituted in place of the recommended plug for an engine. This may temporarily relieve the condition; however, spark plugs cannot take the place of needed engine work.

Carbon Fouling

Soft, black, sooty deposits can easily be identified as carbon fouling. When plugs in this condition are removed from an engine, you should check your catalog before doing anything else. Make sure the correct spark plug was installed by the person doing the previous work. If someone has experimented with a change in heat range and installed a spark plug that is too cold for the engine, carbon fouling may easily result.

If the heat range is correct, carbon fouling can usually be attributed to an over-rich fuel-air mixture caused by a sticking choke or clogged air cleaner. It can also be caused by weak ignition, inoperative preheating system, retarded timing, or low compression.

Carbon fouling could also be the result of slow stop-and-start, short-trip service. If this is the case and all adjustments are correct, a one-step hotter plug may be used to compensate for these operating conditions.

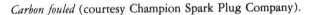

Carbon fouled (courtesy Champion Spark Plug Company).

Worn-out Plugs

Here's a plug that has served its useful life of 10,000 miles or more and should be replaced. The color of the insulator nose indicates that the heat range is correct; deposits are normal, but the electrodes are rounded and worn. The voltage required to spark across the gap has approximately doubled and will continue to increase with additional miles of travel. In short, the plug is worn out.

Worn out (courtesy Champion Spark Plug Company).

Even higher voltage requirements, as much as 100 percent above normal, may occur when the engine is quickly accelerated to wide-open throttle. Spark plugs that misfire noticeably under heavy loads are probably misfiring or tracking unnoticeably during normal driving, wasting power and fuel and increasing emissions of unburned hydrocarbons.

Abnormal Combustion vs. the Spark Plug

Detonation and preignition (see below) are different phenomena, but quite similar in origin. One can incite the other and either is capable of causing severe damage to internal engine components including the spark plug.

The spark plug is rarely the cause; rather it is the victim of abnormal combustion. Because the spark plug is positioned in the combustion chamber, it is readily exposed to the damaging effects of preignition and detonation. The responsibility for piston damage is often unfairly placed on the spark plug simply because it may show evidence of damage similar to that of the piston. There are instances, however, where piston damage may occur with no damage to the spark plug.

All engine and spark plug manufacturers are well aware of abnormal combustion and the extreme stresses it imposes, but they cannot prevent its occurrence when engine adjustments, fuels and/or lubricants vary from their recommendations. Unqualified experimentation or improper servicing of the modern internal-combustion engine is not recommended. To be sure that both performance and service life will not be impaired, always follow the recommended servicing guidelines established for any given engine.

Detonation

Detonation has fractured the insulator core nose of this spark plug. When detonation occurs, a portion of the air/fuel charge will begin to burn spontaneously from increased heat and pressures just after ignition takes place. The resulting "explosion" applies extreme pressures to internal engine components and the increased heat factor can cause preignition.

Detonation can usually be attributed to one or a combination of the following conditions:

1. Ignition timing is advanced too far.
2. Gasoline octane rating is too low.
3. Lean air-fuel mixtures. Poor carburetion and/or leaks in the intake manifold.
4. Compression ratio increase due to combustion chamber deposits or engine modification.
5. Excessive intake manifold temperatures.
6. Lugging the engine.

Detonation (courtesy Champion Spark Plug Company).

Preignition

This plug is a good example of the damage caused by preignition. Note the burned electrodes and blistered insulator. Preignition is just what the term implies—ignition of the fuel charge prior to the time it sparks. Hot spots within the combustion chamber are capable of initiating combustion.

Preignition is usually the result of one or a combination of the following conditions:

1. Combustion chamber deposits which become incandescent.
2. Hot spots in the combustion chamber due to poor control of engine heat.
3. Piston scuffing, due to inadequate lubrication or improper clearance on engine parts.
4. Detonation or conditions leading to it.
5. Cross firing (electrical induction between spark plug wires).
6. Spark plug heat range too high for engine.

Preignition (courtesy Champion Spark Plug Company).

Overheating

Effects of high temperature on the spark plug are usually indicated by a clean white insulator core nose and/or excessive electrode erosion. The insulator may also be blistered.

Check for the correct spark plug heat range. If a plug that is too hot for the engine has been installed, overheating may result. However, over-advanced ignition timing, insufficient cooling system level and/or stop-

Overheated (courtesy Champion Spark Plug Company).

pages, lean air-fuel mixtures, or a leaking intake manifold can overheat the correct spark plug.

If spark plug overheating occurs and all ignition and engine adjustments are known to be correct and no other engine malfunction exists, a heat range one step colder may be necessary to obtain improved service life.

Mechanical Damage

There are three ways that mechanical damage can occur to the firing end of a spark plug. One is as a result of a foreign object in the combustion chamber. Because of valve overlap, it is possible for small objects to migrate

Mechanical damage (courtesy Champion Spark Plug Company).

from one cylinder to another. If mechanical damage is discovered, check the other cylinders to prevent a recurrence of this problem. When working on an engine, keep the carburetor throat and any open plug holes covered to keep out foreign objects.

Mechanical damage can also be caused by the piston. Improper reach plugs, whose threaded section extends into the combustion chamber, may collide with the piston. Even where sufficient clearances may exist, the exposed threads may become the source of preignition. Always consult a recommendation chart for the correct spark plug.

Finally, improper use of electrode gap tools can inflict damage to the plug firing end. Never apply pressure to the insulator core nose section or the center electrode. Obviously, mishandling of spark plugs, as with any engine part, can lead to physical damage.

Combustion Deposits

Combustion deposits that accumulate in the engine do not exclusively collect on the firing end of a spark plug—quite the opposite. They generally gather throughout the combustion chamber area without bias toward any of the parts. The plug firing end simply reflects the atmosphere within which it exists during its useful service life.

There are several forms of combustion deposits that may affect engine performance. How well can you interpret these conditions and identify their causes? Keep in mind these two important facts: (1) The quantity, color or overall appearance of the deposits are not as important as their chemical nature; and (2) the electrical characteristics of the deposits at room temperature will not be the same as at operating temperatures within an engine.

Ash Deposits

Ash deposits, colored light brown to white, may be found encrusted on the side or center electrodes and core nose. They are derived from the burning of oil and/or fuel additives during normal combustion. Normally they are nonconductive; however, excessive amounts may mask the spark, resulting in misfire.

Ash fouled (courtesy Champion Spark Plug Company).

If the deposits prove to be compounds of oil, they may be the result of a seepage of oil past the valve guides and/or piston rings. In due time, consistent exposure to this condition can result in a much heavier deposit.

Corrective measures may include the installation of valve guide seals to prevent oil from seeping into the combustion chamber.

Splash Fouling

Splash fouling in varying degrees appears as spotted deposits on the insulator core nose. Through the course of normal engine service, combus-

Splash fouled (courtesy Champion Spark Plug Company).

tion efficiency deteriorates because of worn ignition parts and retarded timing. By-products of combustion will collect not only on the plugs, but on piston crowns and valves as well. Following a long-delayed tune-up, deposits may suddenly loosen when normal combustion temperatures are restored. During a hard acceleration these materials may shed off the piston and be thrown against the hot insulator surface of the plug. If they happen to short out the plug by providing a track to ground, misfire will occur. These deposits can be removed through regular cleaning techniques and the plugs reinstalled to serve their normal, useful life.

Gap Bridging

Gap bridging does not occur too often in automotive engines. It's associated with the same or similar conditions that produce splash fouling. In this case, however, a chunk of the deposit is thrown loose and lodges between the side and center electrodes, forming an electrical bridge. Result? A "dead short." In a few cases, where fluffy deposits accumulate on the side electrode, these materials may melt and bridge the gap when the engine is suddenly put under heavy load.

Misfire caused by a bridged gap is reasonably easy to locate. The positive fix consists of simply removing the particle from between the electrodes.

A similar bridging effect can occur between the insulator nose and the shell. Identified as core bridging, it, too, can affect engine performance. If not too severe, such deposits can also be easily removed.

Gap bridging (courtesy Champion Spark Plug Company).

Insulator Glazing

Glazing appears as a shiny deposit, yellow or tan in color. The presence of glazing indicates that spark plug temperatures have suddenly risen during a hard, fast acceleration, and normal combustion deposits (which usually don't impair performance) have no opportunity to slough-off. Instead, they melt to form a conductive coating which can cause misfire.

Glazing (courtesy Champion Spark Plug Company).

Carburetors Do Have Problems

We are getting farther and farther away from the days of solving problems by "adjusting them out" at the carburetor. But it is not completely a thing of the past, particularly since there still exist some "vintage" cars with adjustable carburetors, and many cars with after-market carburetors.

And it is entirely possible that the carburetor may need rebuilding. But Andy Guria, of Holley Carburetor Division of Colt Industries, warns drivers to "be sure before you take off the carburetor."

According to Guria, "A service technician's most important tool is a keen sense of observation. This ability is usually acquired through experience and making occasional errors.

"You read in every manual the slogan, 'Test, don't guess.' The beginner's first impulse is to 'tear' something apart. The real problem is far more difficult to find after everything is disassembled.

"At least fifty to seventy-five percent of the layman-owner's carburetor problems can be cured without touching the carburetor except for a possible idle mixture and speed adjustment," he says.

It may surprise you to hear that the average driver cannot detect a miss in one cylinder. While driving down the highway at 50–70 mph the car runs reasonably well. When the driver pulls up to a stop signal and returns to an idle condition, the engine idles rough.

"The driver goes to his favorite service facility and complains of a rough idle," says Guria. "Here's where an attempt to adjust the idle will probably do more harm than good.

"Starting in 1968 the under-hood temperatures were increased tremendously. The insulation on secondary wiring would not withstand the higher temperature. On one particular application the Holley service representatives have had numerous complaints of rough idle. Nearly all of these complaints could be corrected by replacing the number seven and/or number eight spark plug wire and then properly readjusting the idle.

"Another common complaint that is hard to define is flooding. Most of the flooding complaints received by Holley service representatives are *not* flooding.

"Gasoline, unlike water which boils at two hundred and twelve degrees Fahrenheit at sea level, boils at many temperatures. The IBP [initial boiling point] of gasoline is usually somewhere between ninety-five and a hundred degrees. The fifty percent point, the temperature at which fifty percent of the fuel boils away is somewhere between a hundred eighty-five and two hundred twenty-five degrees.

"After the engine is shut off, the under-hood temperature begins to rise. When the engine has been shut off for twenty minutes, referred to as a "hot soak" period, the temperature will usually reach its peak. This condition will occur particularly in the summertime or when the car is stored in a heated or attached garage.

"Fuel will frequently drip from the ends of the throttle shaft or can be observed dripping out of the main discharge nozzle or pump nozzle into the manifold. There are two annoying results. First, fuel vapors or fumes will be noticed if the owner has a basement under or attached garage next to the kitchen. Second, hard, hot starting occurs if the driver attempts to start the car after it has stood for twenty minutes.

"This condition is *percolation,* not flooding," Guria explains.

Flooding is a condition that occurs when the fuel level is not properly attained, the float is rubbing on the side of the fuel bowl, or the fuel inlet needle is held off the seat by some foreign matter or it is not properly seating due to wear.

"A classic example of percolation was recorded recently," says Guria. "A lady driver stopped frequently at an ice cream store to buy ice cream. When she bought a quart of vanilla and returned to her car the car started instantly. When she purchased butter pecan and returned to her car it wouldn't start.

"An alert service representative made two trips to the store with the driver. The first trip she bought vanilla. It was prepacked and she returned to the car in five minutes and the vehicle started perfectly. When she returned to buy the butter pecan she waited twenty minutes for it to be hand packed and to pay her bill. When she returned to the car she pumped the accelerator two or three times, adding additional fuel to the already over-rich mixture in the manifold. The car wouldn't start. It was necessary for the representative to explain the correct procedure to start a hot engine. Most new cars today have instructions on the sun visor explaining the proper starting procedure for a hot and a cold engine."

However, carburetors *do* need service and there are carburetor problems.

Many of the real carburetor problems are the result of increasingly high under-hood temperatures. The higher temperature heating and cooling cycles accelerate the formation of gum and varnish and relax the torque of carburetor mounting bolts and assembly screws. Due to the heat cycling, gaskets are compressed and can take a set allowing vacuum leaks to occur. This is especially true where preemission-type carburetors are used in emission-oriented applications and subjected to greater heat and stress than that for which they were originally designed.

"We are acquainted with two owners who live next door to each other," says Guria. "They both drive cars of the same make and engine size. One owner trades his car every two years after seventy-five thousand miles. The other drives five thousand miles a year; five miles to the village to pick up his *Wall Street Journal* and have coffee and donuts at the village restaurant. Each carburetor requires cleaning and rebuilding once a year. It is far more difficult to remove the gum and varnish formation from the idle and high-speed bleeds, the venturi, and the throttle bore of the carburetor that has only been driven five thousand miles."

There is a lot of kidding about buying a used car that was driven by a nice old lady from Pasadena. Your better buy might be a car that has reasonably high mileage on it and has been properly serviced.

If you are a beginner in tune-up and carburetor service, start with the simple jobs. The car that has been to every shop in town will have every rod and every adjustment fouled up and will require the attention of a qualified expert technician or a new carburetor.

And, before condemning or removing the carburetor, be sure there *is* a carburetor problem. Therefore, preliminary evaluation and diagnosis is most important.

Since 1968 there have been a series of engine modifications as well as carburetor modifications. These modifications are interrelated. The valve overlap, manifold modifications, valve location, combustion chamber design, and reduced compression ratio have made the service of the ignition system a necessary part of carburetor care.

If you were to remove one spark plug wire, your first thought would be that the emissions would be increased ⅛, or 12½ percent. Not so, the total emissions would be increased anywhere from 90 to 135 percent.

Maladjustment of ignition timing by as much as 5 degrees retard, on some recent-model vehicles equipped with the latest emission control systems, may result in sluggish engine responsiveness, stalls on cold engine vehicle driveaways, and poor fuel economy.

Manifold Vacuum Leaks

The manifold mounting bolts and carburetor mounting nuts or cap screws should be tightened at 4,000 to 6,000 miles. A liquid leak detector is available at all parts supply points or one can be made by mixing engine oil with kerosene or cleaning solvent. Squirt the fluid around the manifold edges with a squirt oil can. Engine speed-up will confirm a leak and the movement of the liquid will indicate the leak's location.

A manifold vacuum leak results in a lean misfire, increasing emissions, and a flame that could cause an engine fire.

Carburetor Metering Systems

There are four basic metering systems in all popular U.S. automotive carburetors: the idle system, main metering system, accelerator pump system, and power enrichment system. In addition, all U.S.-built carburetors have a fuel inlet or float system and a choke system.

The idle or idle transfer system supplies a comparatively rich mixture for curb idle and a leaner mixture for low-speed operation.

The main metering system supplies the leanest mixture for cruising in approximately the 35–70 mph range. Enough air (oxygen) is supplied through the venturi to insure nearly complete combustion of the air-fuel mixture.

When the vehicle is accelerated, air (being lighter than fuel) rushes in to fill the demand. The gasoline takes a short period of time to "catch up" to the air and supply a combustible mixture. The pump system, whether a diaphragm or piston type, mechanically supplies additional fuel to the engine to prevent a stall or stumble when the throttle is opened rapidly.

The power enrichment system supplies a richer mixture for heavy load or full power. Most modern power systems are vacuum-operated and begin to supply additional fuel to the main metering system when engine vacuum drops to the area of 5–10 inches of vacuum. This enrichment provides maximum power for the particular carburetor manifold and prevents exhaust valve burning.

The fuel inlet system, which includes the fuel inlet valve and float, maintains the correct fuel level in the fuel bowl. The fuel level is an important part of the metering system.

The choke system supplies a rich mixture to start the engine when cold and a slightly richer than normal mixture for cold driveaway. Choke systems may be of three types: The simplest is a hand choke operated by a knob on the dash; a divorced choke is mounted in a heat sink in the inlet manifold; an integral choke is mounted on the carburetor and the bimetal is heated by means of a heat tube from the exhaust manifold. Any of these chokes may have electric heating elements to speed up the "choke off" interval. When the engine starts, the original "pull off" (qualifying) or opening is done with a vacuum diaphragm or piston.

Carburetor Removal or Adjustment?

Before deciding that the carburetor needs to be removed, you should make every adjustment possible. If this doesn't help your carburetor problems, then you may well need to replace—or better (cheaper?) yet—rebuild it. But first buy a service manual for your car's particular brand of carburetor and make all of the adjustments you can. The Holley Service Guide, for example, sells for only a few dollars and covers every carburetor in the Holley line. Other manufacturers have similar manuals.

Make adjustments according to directions in the manual. Be sure the manual covers the steps for rebuilding your particular carburetor model, and have the proper rebuilding *kit* on hand. The latter is particularly important; a rebuilding kit is not expensive, and if you are going to the trouble of taking it all apart, you should replace every diaphragm, seal, and gasket.

With manual in hand and all possible adjustments attempted, you can now take off the carburetor.

The first step in removing the carburetor is to take out the air cleaner. Late-model air cleaners usually have two or more connecting hoses or tubes. A large-diameter hose or tube connects the air cleaner with the shroud around the exhaust manifold. This hot-air duct may be more easily disconnected at the shroud than at the air cleaner. The normal procedure is to wipe the air cleaner pan clean with a solvent-dampened shop towel, and clean up road dust and deposits.

You will probably find it easier to disconnect the small vacuum line from the air cleaner than from the base of the carburetor. In fact, you may discover that the vacuum hose has been left loose from the air cleaner by someone who has previously removed it. This may cause a lean idle roughness or "off idle" hesitation similar to other vacuum leaks. After the carburetor has been removed, you can carefully remove this hose.

As mentioned previously, a good tune-up technician's most important tool is a keen sense of observation. Carefully check every tube in the emission system. Cracked, broken, or split tubes must be replaced, not with just any old tubing; the replacement tubing must be of a heat-resistant type. Split or broken tubing cannot be permanently repaired with plastic electrical tape. One small import has twenty-one hoses or connections that must be disconnected before the carburetor can be removed.

Remove the carburetor-attaching nuts or cap screws. Note whether they are tight or loose.

The carburetor is frequently stuck to the manifold flange gasket. Don't pry on the carburetor. This may bend or break the mounting lugs or ears. Carefully tap the throttle flange from side to side with a plastic hammer to loosen the carburetor from the flange gasket.

Disassembly

Install the carburetor on a stand or use some other means to keep it off the bench. If you drop the carburetor on a work bench, the throttle valves may be badly nicked or dislocated. A nick can cause the throttle valve to stick. A dislocated throttle valve will change the idle port, EGR port, and distributor vacuum port relationship. Remove the idle solenoid, choke diaphragm, choke housing, secondary diaphragm, or dashpot if these are part of the carburetor.

These elements should be wiped clean with a shop towel dampened in cleaning solvent. They should never be immersed in commercial carburetor cleaner or solvent.

Some fuel inlet nuts or fittings have a tendency to seize or stick in the threaded zinc or aluminum fuel bowls or covers. After the fuel line nut has been removed, the inlet fitting can frequently be loosened more easily while the carburetor is still mounted on the engine. Install the proper size wrench on the fitting and tap gently with a plastic hammer.

Tune-up for Performance and Economy

Inspection

Inspection is a part of disassembly. Be curious. If a part has a dark or shiny area, check the fit. If the casting looks suspicious, check the trueness with a straightedge.

Note: While you are disassembling the carburetor, follow the complete procedure under each model.

Cleaning

Cleaning is a most important part of carburetor service. The correct parts and assembly, proper torque, and exact adjustments are meaningless unless the air-bleeds, venturi, throttle body, and all passages are free of gum, varnish, or dirt.

Complete cleaning is done in three steps. After the carburetor has been disassembled, rinse off the rough dirt in a bucket or pan of solvent.

The gum and varnish may be removed with lacquer thinner or commercial-grade acetone and a cleaning brush and shop towel. Finish the cleaning with air as explained later on.

The three-stage cleaning is done in the following manner:

First, the very small parts are placed in a fine mesh basket or a small tin can with several holes punched in the bottom. The main body, bowl cover, throttle body, and other submersible parts are placed in the large basket and all the parts submersed in a good commercial carburetor cleaner for thirty minutes. Exterior dirt and gum may need an assist with a brush.

After removing, place the basket and parts in a can of cleaning solvent. Either agitate the basket or dunk it up and down to thoroughly rinse the parts.

The third step is a thorough dunking in hot water (just below the boiling point). Leave the parts in the water until they are thoroughly heated. When thoroughly heated, they will air-dry immediately after the basket is removed from the water.

All passages in all parts should be blown out with compressed air. Never use wires or drills.

Reassembly

Reassembly is essentially the reverse of disassembly. In fact, in military carburetor manuals, each photograph is numbered in two sequences.

Note: There are four things to watch on reassembly: Do you have the right parts? Do you have the right gaskets? Are you assembling the parts in the correct order? Are the screws and bolts properly torqued? For example, all throttle-body screws are torqued to 50 in. lb. and most bowl cover screws are torqued to 30 in. lbs. All screws should be torqued in three stages, in a criss-cross pattern.

Any special precautions will be covered in the manual under each carburetor model.

On Fuel Economy

Once you have performed the tune-ups suggested in this chapter, it is pretty much up to you as the driver to add the final ingredient, if fuel economy is what you are after. This, obviously, refers to highway driving, because if you have to worry about *economy* on the race track, you had better not be there in the first place. Racing and economy—like Scotch and tonic—just don't mix.

So what is this ingredient you can add to improve economy? Simple. Smoothness. It is the key to driving race cars *fast,* and it is the key to getting more miles per gallon.

Do everything smoothly. Accelerate smoothly and slowly. Brake smoothly; don't wait too long and then jump on the brakes. Steer smoothly and look ahead, planning your lane changes and road position *before* you have to change lanes or position.

Watch the accelerator. Every carburetor has an accelerator pump, most with four jets the size of a ballpoint pen tip. When you jump on the throttle, those jets squirt out raw gas under pressure, so remember that fire-hose effect every time you stand on it.

As for driving in hilly terrain, allow the car to roll a little faster downhill, then let it slow below the speed limit going uphill. Keep the throttle steady. Smoothness again. But don't slow it up so much that the automatic transmission downshifts or the standard shift lugs, or you'll be using more gas. The same is true for rounding curves. If your car is set up properly, you can maintain steady speeds through all but the tightest of corners.

Somebody once said that if you drove as if you had an uncooked egg between your foot and the accelerator pedal, your gas mileage would be increased significantly. No doubt. But you don't have to go overboard. You can still enjoy motoring and get maximum mileage if your car is set up properly in the first place and is kept well-maintained and tuned after that. Just how economical you want to be at this point depends entirely on how far into the carburetor you place your foot.

10

Driving Schools

Is experience alone enough to teach you to drive well at high speed? Probably. If you have the patience.

But you can learn a whole lot faster—and better—if you enroll in one of the better driving schools throughout the country. A good school can save you as much as five years of trial-and-error techniques on the race track or highway. Without doubt, you can apply the techniques from the preceding chapters to your own personal driving program, and you will drive better. Much better. After all, nobody taught Bob Bondurant how to drive a race car and he became one of the greats, so it all boils down to just how impatient you are.

Having driven race cars for years, I was smugly confident, but I will be the first to admit that Bondurant and instructor Bill Cooper greatly improved my lap times *and* my confidence.

The major difference between Bondurant's school and most of the others is that he uses sedans and sports cars in addition to formula cars. In other words, at the Bondurant School you can improve your highway driving as well as your racing skills. But that may be a moot point, because most people who go to driving schools go there to learn to *race*. Pity. A lot of highway drivers could use some instruction.

The Skip Barber School offers a complete race series—an opportunity to put your knowledge to use immediately, in one of his cars. And, too, Barber has schools at many locations throughout the East and Midwest.

The Bertil Roos School at the Pocono International Raceway differs from the others in that Roos teaches it all himself; the Scotti School in Massachusetts teaches only defensive driving, and the E. Paul Dickinson School in Huntington, West Virginia, teaches solo competition. Dickinson, by the way, is a five-time national solo champion and has never been defeated in national competition.

Prices range from a few hundred dollars for a one- or two-day course to $5,000 for the complete Barber race series, so your pursestrings may have a lot to do with your choice.

Following regular instruction at the Skip Barber School, you can enter the race series, which truly offers a chance for an inexperienced driver to develop his skills rapidly under ideal circumstances. Instead of juggling car problems, the new racer can turn his full attention to speed and tactics.

The series also gives the experienced driver an opportunity to upgrade his level of performance, and to evaluate his competitive position apart from the differences in car preparation and check-writing abilities.

But more than anything, it's a chance for any determined driver to compete against drivers with similar skills and to enjoy terrific racing in a competitive car at a remarkably low cost.

Forget all of the problems of owning a race car—purchase, development, maintenance, towing, insurance, testing, trick motors, and so on. The Skip Barber series provides a race-ready car—one that could go out and win a regional competition. These are all Crossle 32Fs, the most successful Formula Ford on today's market. Most important, all the cars in this mini-IROC are absolutely in top condition and are competitive equals. But should one break or become uncompetitive, spares are always on hand.

And you get to drive in fourteen races during the season, plus practice sessions and continued individual appraisal from the instructors. The cost of the program includes the car and all expenses, except personal ones, of course. And who in his right mind would consider covering any racer's *personal* expenses?

Here is a list of the major driving schools in North America:

Skip Barber Racing School
1000 Massachusetts Ave.
Boxboro, MA 01719
617/263-3771

Bob Bondurant School of High Performance Driving
Highways 37 and 121
Sonoma, CA 95476
707/938-4741

Driving Schools

British School of Motor Racing
3901 East G St.
Ontario, CA 91761
714/983-0551

E. Paul Dickinson Solo (Autocross) School
819 Tenth Ave.
Huntington, WV 25701
304/529-7516

Road Atlanta Driver Training Center
Rt. 1
Braselton, GA 30517
404/967-6143

Bertil Roos School of Motor Racing
Box 221-A
Blakeslee, PA 18610
717/646-7227

Jim Russell International Racing Driver's School
P.O. Box 911
Rosamond, CA 93560
805/256-2715

Jim Russell International Racing Driver's School, Canada*
Box 119-AC9
Mt. Tremblant, Quebec JOT IZO
819/425-2739

Bill Scott Racing School
1420 Spring Hill Rd.
McLean, VA 22101
703/893-3992

Scotti School of Defensive Driving
P.O. Box 59
Somerville, MA 02144
617/776-8590

*Not affiliated with Jim Russell, Rosamond, CA.

Appendix:
Specific Cars by Class

Showroom Stock Category

SSA Class

Alfa Romeo Spider 2000, 5-spd
Alfa Romeo Spring Veloce, 5-spd
AMC AMX 304, 4-spd
Chevrolet Monza 2+2, Spyder, 305,
    4-spd
Datsun 280Z, 4-spd
Datsun 280ZX, 4–5-spd
Ford Mustang II, Mach L, Cobra II,
    302, 4-spd
Ford Mustang, 302, 4-spd, W/TRX
    package
Ford Mustang, Turbo 2, 3, 4-spd,
    W/TRX package
Ford Mustang, Pace Car 302
Ford Mustang, Pace Car 2.3 Turbo
Mazda RX-4 (77, 2-dr, 77–78, 4-dr)
Mazda RX-7, S, GS, 4–5-spd
Mercury Capri RS, 302, 4-spd,
    W/TRX package
Mercury Capri RS, Turbo 2.3, 4-spd
    W/TRX package
Porsche 924, 4-spd
Saab Turbo "99"
Saab Turbo "900"

SSB Class

Alfa Romeo Alfetta
Alfa Romeo Alfetta GT
AMC Gremlin & "X," 258, 4-spd
AMC Spirit, DL, GT Liftback, 258,
    4-spd
BMW 320i
Buick Skylark 231 cid
Datsun 200 SX
Fiat 124 Spyder
Fiat X1/9, 1500, 5-spd
Fiat 131, 2-dr, 4-dr
Fiat Spider 2000, 5-spd
Fiat Brava, 2000, 5-spd
Ford Mustang II, Mach I, Cobra II

Ford Mustang V6, 4-spd, W-Rally
   package
Honda Accord, 1751, 5-spd
Mazda RX-3 SP, RX-3
Mercury Capri II, 2300
Mercury Capri II, V6
Mercury Capri, V6, 4-spd, W/Rally
   package
Oldsmobile Starfire, V6

Plymouth Arrow & GT 2000 (77–78,
   4-spd) (79, 5-spd)
SAAB 99, L, GL
SAAB 900 GLi, 4-spd
Triumph TR-7, 5-spd, coupe & conv.
Toyota Celica, ST, GT, GT Liftback
VW Scirocco, 4-spd
VW Rabbit, 4-spd

SSC Class

AMC Gremlin & Gremlin "X," 258,
   3-spd
AMC Pacer & "X," 258, 3-spd
Buick Opel Isuzu, std, Delux, 4-spd
Buick Opel Isuzu, S/C, 4–5-spd
Chevrolet Chevette & Scooter, 1.4, 1.6
Chevrolet Monza, 2300
Chevrolet Monza, 2474 cc
Chevrolet Vega, 140
Chevrolet Vega, 140 GT
Datsun 210
Datsun 310
Datsun 510
Datsun B210
Datsun 710
Dodge Colt, 2-dr
Dodge Colt Hatchback, 1.6 (split
   shift)
Dodge Omni, 4-dr
Dodge Omni, 024
Fiat 128 Sedan

Fiat X 1/9, 1300, 4-spd
Fiat Strada, 1500, 5-spd
Ford Fiesta, std, Ghia & Sport
Ford Pinto, 2300, Pony 78
Ford Pinto, 2-dr, 3-dr, Pony, W/Rally
   or ESS package
Honda Civic, CVCC
Honda Accord
Mazda GLC
Mercury Bobcat, 2.3
Plymouth Horizon, 4-dr
Plymouth Horizon, TC3
Plymouth Arrow 160 & GT
Plymouth Champ 1.6 (split shift)
Pontiac Astre 2300 or 2474
Renault R5, GL, GTL
Subaru (all)
Toyota Corolla (all)
VW Rabbit F.I., std W/145-13, C &
   L W/155–13, 4-spd

GT Category

Class GT-1

AMC Concord
AMC Gremlin 2-dr Sedan
AMC Hornet
AMC Javelin 1968
AMC Javelin 1969
AMC Javelin AMX 1970
AMC Pacer

AMC AMX
AMC Spirit
Buick Century
Buick Regal
Buick Skyhawk/Skylark
Chevrolet Camero 1967–69
Chevrolet Camero 1970

Appendix: Specific Cars by Class

Chevrolet Chevelle
Chevrolet Malibu
Chevrolet Monte Carlo
Chevrolet Monza
Chevrolet Monza Mirage
Chevrolet Nova 1972
Dodge Aspen
Dodge Challenger T/A 1970
Dodge Dart 273
Ford Cobra II
Ford Fairmont
Ford Granada
Ford Mustang 1973
Ford Mustang H.T. 1965–66
Ford Mustang H.T. 1967–68
Ford Mustang Fastback H.T. 1969
Ford Mustang Boss 302 1969
Ford Mustang 1970
Ford Mustang II 302
Ford Mustang V-6 & V-8
Ford Mustang 2.3 Turbo
Mercury Capri 2.3 Turbo RS
Mercury Capri V-6 & V-8
Mercury Cougar 1967
Mercury Monarch
Mercury Zephyr
Oldsmobile Cutlass
Oldsmobile Starfire
Plymouth Barracuda 1968
Plymouth Barracuda 1969
Plymouth AAR 'Cuda
Plymouth Valiant
Plymouth Volare
Pontiac Firebird (1968) 1970
Pontiac Firebird, Trans-Am 1970

Pontiac Grand Am
Pontiac Grand Prix
Pontiac GTO 1964
Pontiac LeMans
Pontiac Sunbird
Pontiac Trans-Am 1969
Saab Turbo
Abarth Simca 2000
AMX Sports Coupe 200, thru 1969
AMX Sports Coupe 343, thru 1969
AMX Sports Coupe 390, 1969 and
   1970
Corvette 283, 327
Corvette 1978 Indy and 1979–80
   Corvette
Corvette Sting Ray Roadster & Coupe
   327, 350, 1963–77
Corvette Sting Ray Roadster & Coupe
   396, 427, 454, thru 1974
De Tomaso Pantera
Ferrari 275 GTB
Ferrari 308 GTB
Ferrari 365 GTB 4 Daytona
Ford Boss 429 Mustang 1969 and
   1970
Jaguar Series 3E
Jaguar XJ-S
Porsche 911 SC Coupe/Targa,
   1973–77
Porsche 911 SC 3.0 Liter
Porsche Turbo Carrera
Porsch Turbo Carrera 3.3 Liter
Shelby Cobra 289
Shelby GT 350, 1965–67, & 1969
Shelby Cobra 427

Class GT-2

Alfa Romeo 1750/2000 TI Berlina
Alfa Romeo 1750/2000 GTV
Alfetta 2000
Alfetta GT 2000
BMW 320i
BMW 2000 TI
BMW 2002 and 2002 TI
Chevrolet Vega
Cosworth Vega

Chrysler Colt 2000
Datsun PL 510
Datsun 510 '80
Datsun 510 1800
Datsun 610
Datsun 710
Datsun 810
Datsun 200 SX
Datsun 200 SX '80

Fiat 131 & Brava
Ford Capri 2000
Ford Capri 2.3L (non Turbo)
Ford Pinto 2000 & 2300
Ford Mustang II 2300
Ford Mustang III 2.3L (non Turbo)
Mazda RX-2
Mazda S124 A RX-3
Opel Rallye Kadett
Opel 1900 Sport Coupe (57R)

Opel 1900 Models 51 & 53
Saab 99 E. CM, LE, EMS, GL
Toyota Celica 2000 & 2189
Toyota Celica Liftback & Sports
Coupe
Volvo P-544
Volvo 122S
Volvo 142S and 142E
Volvo 242/244 DL

Class GT-3

Alfa Romeo GTV 1600
Auto Union Audi Fox
BMW 1600-2 and 1602
Chrysler Colt
Chrysler Colt Coupe
Chrysler Dodge Omni & 024
Datsun 510 1600
Datsun B210 1300
Datsun B210 1400
Datsun F-10
Datsun 310 1400
Fiat 124 Sport Coupe 1438
Fiat 124 Sport Coupe 1608
Fiat 124 Special
Fiat 138
Fiat 131 Coupe & Sedan
Ford Cortina GT 1499/1598, 1967
Ford Lotus Cortina TC 1964/65/66

Ford Lotus Cortina TC 1967
Ford Escort Mexico
Ford Capri 1600
Ford Pinto 1600
Ford Fiesta
Honda Civic CVCC 1438
Plymouth Horizon & TCS
Renault 12
Renault 17TS
Saab Sedan V4 1498 & 1598
Toyota Corolla 1600
Toyota Corolla Liftback & Sport
Coupe
Toyota Carina 1600
VW 1500/1600 1967/68/69
VW 1600 1970
VW Rabbit, Scirocco 1471, 1588

Class GT-4

Alfa Romeo Guilia 1300 & 1300 TI
Alfa Romeo Junior 1300 GTA
Austin America 1275
Austin/Morris 850
Austin/Morris Mini-Cooper 997
Austin/Morris Mini-Cooper 998
Austin/Morris Mini-Cooper "S" 1097
Austin/Morris Mini-Cooper 1275
Datsun B (L) 100 (L200)
Fiat 600D
Fiat 850 Sport Coupe
Fiat 124 1200
Fiat 128
Fiat 128 SL Coupe 13-0 and 3P

Ford Escort Super and 1300 GT
Ford New Anglia 997 and Ford
123/124E
Anglia Super 1200
Honda Civic 1179 and 1237
NSU-1000 (SU-TTS)
NSU TT1200
Renault 8-R1130 & R1132
Renault R8 Major R1132
Renault R8 Gordini R1135
Renault 5 & LeCar R1229
Saab 96 Sedan
Simca 1000 Type SD
Sunbeam IMP/Singer Chamois

Toyota Corolla 1100   VW 1300 1965/66
Toyota Corolla 1200   VW 1300 1967

Production Category

Class C

Alfa Romeo Giulia TZ
Alfa Romeo Montreal
Datsun 240Z, 260Z, & 280Z thru
 1977
Datsun 280Z 2+2
Datsun 280ZX
Jaguar Xk-E 3.8 & r.2 Coupe &
 Roadster
Mazda RX7
Lotus Elan 1600, S-2, S-4, Roadster,
 Coupe & Drophead
Lotus Elan Plus 2
Lotus Europa Twin Cam
Lotus Espirit
Porsche 924 Turbo

Porsche 911 T, E, S Coupe/Targa
 1969–1977
Porsche 914/6
Porsche 912 Coupe/Targa thru 1968
Porsche 912 Coupe/Targa 1969
Porsche 912 E
Porsche 914/4
Sunbeam Tiger 260
Triumph TR-6 (F.I.)
Triumph TR-8
Triumph TR-8 (F.I.)
Triumph TR-2, 3, 3A, 3B
Triumph TR-4, TR-4A
Triumph TR-4A IRS
TVR MK III 1622

Class D

Alfa Romeo Spider 2000 & Veloce
 thru 1979
Austin-Healey 3000 MK I, II, III
Daimler SP 250
Datsun SRL 311U
Elva Courier MK III 1800, & MK IV
 1800
Elva Courier MK IV, T Roadster &
 Coupe
Jaguar XK 120, 140, 150, 3.4 & 3.8
Jensen-Healey & GT
Lotus Super Seven
Lotus Seven Series Four

MGC & MGC GT
Porsche Carrea 1500, 1600
Porsche 911, L, T. S Coupe/Targa
 thru 1968
Porsche 914S
Porsche 924
Triumph-GT-6, GT-6+
Triumph GT-6, MK III thru 1972
Triumph GT-6, MK III 1973–1974
Triumph TR-250, TR-6 (SU)
Triumph TR-7 Coupe and Convertible
TVR MK III 1800
Yenko Stinger Coupe

Class E

Alfa Romeo Giulia Spider Veloce
Alfa Romeo Giulia Sprint & GTC
Alfa Romeo Spider Duetto & 1750
 Spider thru 1971
Austin-Healey BN 4, BN 6 (100-6)

Elva Courier MK I, II, III, 1622
Elva Courier MK IV, 1622
Fiat 124 Sport Spider 1600 (2
 Carburetor) & 124 Sport Spider
 2000

Lotus Mark 46, 54, 65 Europa
MGB & MGB-GT
Morgan + 4
Opel GT 1900 Model 77
Porsche 356 A, B, C, 1500 & 1600,
 6/1600 SC, B Super 90 and
 Cabriolet
Porsche 912 Coupe/Targa thru 1968

Porsche 912 Coupe/Targa 1969
Porsche 912E
Porsche 914/4
Triumph TR-2, 3, 3A, 3B
Triumph TR-4, TR-4A
Triumph TR-4A IRS
TVR MK III 1622

Class F

Alfa Romeo Giulietta, Super Sprint &
 Spider
Alfa Romeo Giulietta, Sprint Speciale
 & Zagato
Alfa Romeo Giulia Sprint & Spider
Alpine A-110, 1100
Austin-Healey Sprite MK IV 1275
Austin-Healey BN 1, BN 2 (100-4),
 (100M)
Fiat 124 Sport Spider, thru 1979
Fiat Abarth OT 1300/124 Coupe

Fiat X 1/9 1500
Lotus 7+7 America
MG Midget MK III & IV 1275 1500
Morgan 4/4 MK V
Saab Sonett V-4, 97 Sonett III
Sunbeam Alpine
Triumph Spitfire MK III 1296
Triumph Spitfire MK IV and 1500
Turner 1500
Volvo P1800, 1800S & 1800 ES Sports
 Coupe

Glass G

Alfa Romeo Giulietta Sprint, Spider
Alfa Romeo Spider 1300 Junior
Alfa Romeo Junior Z
Austin-Healey Sprite 1100, AN8
 (1100)
Datsun SPL 310 U
Datsun SPL 311, SPL 311 U
Fiat X1/9

Fiat 124 Spider 1438
MGA 1500, 1600, 1622
MGA Twin Cam
MG Midget AN2, AN3
Porsche 1300
Triumph Spitfire, Spitfire Mk II
Turner 950 S

Class H

Austin-Healey Sprite Mk I, Mk II
 (948)
Fiat 850 Spider, Racer, thru 1973
Fiat 850 S Record Monza, 750 GT,

750 Millie Miglia
MG Midget 948
Morgan 4/4 Mk IV
Opel GT 1100